A History of Economic Change
in England, 1880–1939

OPUS 34 *Oxford Paperbacks University Series*

R. S. SAYERS

A History of Economic Change in England, 1880-1939

London
OXFORD UNIVERSITY PRESS
New York Toronto
1967

Oxford University Press, Ely House, London W.1

GLASGOW   NEW YORK   TORONTO   MELBOURNE   WELLINGTON
CAPE TOWN   SALISBURY   IBADAN   NAIROBI   LUSAKA   ADDIS ABABA
BOMBAY   CALCUTTA   MADRAS   KARACHI   LAHORE   DACCA
KUALA LUMPUR   HONG KONG   TOKYO

PRINTED IN GREAT BRITAIN AT THE UNIVERSITY PRESS, OXFORD
BY VIVIAN RIDLER, PRINTER TO THE UNIVERSITY

To T. S. A.

Preface

A BOOK ON THIS SMALL SCALE on this vast subject is necessarily highly selective, and in making my selection both of factual material and of discussion I have based my judgement on the assumption that my most numerous readers will be sixth-formers and first-year university students and that it will be the first book rather than the last they read in this field.

Since all such efforts are inescapably coloured by personal prejudices and the accidents of personal knowledge, I should mention that I lived through more than half the period; no doubt it will all look rather different in the eyes of more detached later generations. In the main I have concentrated on developments in England and Wales, but for some aspects—notably foreign trade—the statistical material has driven me to write in terms of the United Kingdom (which itself changed its area during these decades). I have drawn freely on many of the books named in the Note on Further Reading, as well as contemporary newspapers and periodicals. I must acknowledge particularly my debt to the *Abstract of British Historical Statistics* by B. R. Mitchell and Phyllis Deane (Cambridge, 1962), without which my groundwork would have been altogether heavier. For the sake of overseas readers, I have included a map on which I believe is marked every place in Britain mentioned in the text.

The University of Sydney has allowed me to reproduce, in Chapter 2, most of the R. C. Mills Lecture I gave in 1965. My colleague, Professor A. H. John, helped substantially in the preparation of the Note on Further Reading. Miss A. M. Taylor applied a critical eye to every sentence and has checked the proofs. Miss E. A. Baseden took the main burden of preparing the printer's copy. To all these my warm thanks.

Professor T. S. Ashton has borne a greater burden of responsibility, for he instigated the project, he has read each chapter as it emerged, and he has given the encouragement vital to a reluctant and halting author. It is in acknowledgement of all this as well as of a friendship stretching back over many years that I have, with his permission, dedicated this little book to him.

R. S. S.

February 1967

Contents

1

The English People, 1880-1939

WHEN SIR ROBERT GIFFEN LOOKED BACK over the changes in the British economy in the nineteenth century, he called it 'the statistical century'. He had done as much as anyone to make it so, and thanks to him and to others whose results he was collating, the task of the economic historian becomes quite different when he passes from the England of the Industrial Revolution to the period in which the industrial lead was lost. The statistics at his command range over an altogether wider field, and statistical series that are highly conjectural for earlier periods become reasonably firm. There are, of course, traps in this: the first figures of any statistical series are notoriously unreliable, and Giffen's century was, as he was emphasizing, one in which many of the series had their beginnings. Moreover, statistics are deceptively selective. Political problems—including the collection of taxes—are the great breeders of statistics, and it is all too easy for the historian, with his leaning towards ascertained fact, to give undue prominence to the statistical record and to overlook those mute inglorious Miltons who, because they were no problem for statesmen, found no place in the figures totted up by officers of government.

The century that Giffen surveyed impressed those who wrote of it as a century of progress and of peace. The progress of the British economy—and progress was a fashionable word when Giffen was writing—had scarcely been chequered by Britain's colonial wars or by the Crimean war. In the period 1880-1939, however, the long peace was broken, not so much by the South African war—though this had psychological importance—as by the European tensions that gave rise to comparatively large expenditure on armaments in the early twentieth century and culminated in the war of 1914-18. In economic terms this was the most disturbing war for centuries; the international upset left its mark on several years after the end of the war, and the economic world had scarcely adjusted itself to peace when new tensions developed to preface the 1939 war. To whatever part of the British economy we look in detail, the impact of these wars and rumours of wars is a considerable part of the picture. More generally, these interferences with the processes of economic growth distort the statistician's view. And more damagingly, the economic upsets that could be ascribed to war obscured more deeply seated economic trends from the eyes of those who had responsibilities in economic policy. In short, as compared with the long peace after Waterloo, the six decades after 1880 form a period in which the economic trends were more difficult for the contemporary economic physicians to recognize, and remain more treacherous for us to assess.

Of the population changes we know much, though even on this subject the increasing elaboration of statistics is marred by the wartime break, in 1941, in the decennial census. As in many other aspects of this phase in British economic development, the first impression is of continuation of the great Victorian upward sweep into the first years of the twentieth century, followed by a major change of trend; but equally as we find elsewhere, closer examination reveals underlying change already at the end of the nineteenth century, foreshadowing the more obvious changes that were laid bare after the First World War. In Great Britain there were nearly 30 million people in 1881, and nearly 47 millions in 1940. In absolute terms, the huge decennial increases that had characterized Victorian Britain reached their maximum in 1901-11, at nearly 4 millions, but the *rate* of increase was declining quite fast. The rate of growth of population resulted from the balance of three factors: the birth-rate (which was falling), the death-rate (in which there was an equally spectacular fall), and the quite sizeable emigration. In only the last of these three was the real downturn after 1911, and the persistence of important new trends from the late nineteenth century onwards, in all these three factors, had by 1939 substantially altered the composition of the population by age and by sex.

The decline in the birth-rate can be traced back to the restriction of family size among married couples born about 1850: the people who were having families in roughly the last quarter of the nineteenth century. The change is generally associated with the spread of knowledge of new methods of birth control. This is certainly an important part of the story, but the phenomenon has to be regarded in the light of many other changes in a broad social framework. Changes in economic organization were reducing the importance of the family as an earning unit, while Factory Acts and Education Acts—and the underlying ideas of which such legislation was an expression—were extending the length of time through which children were an unrelieved expense to their parents. However we weigh the various causes that contributed to this great social change, there is no doubt about its manifestation: among the English people the typical family came, by the 1930s, to have one or two children instead of the five, six, or seven of earlier generations. The families of more than six children, once so common in all classes of the community, virtually disappeared. When *The Barretts of Wimpole Street* captured English theatre audiences in the inter-war years, the diminutive 'Occy' (for Octavius) puzzled a generation that rarely needed to name an eighth child; and the 'crocodile', once the family out for its Sunday walk, was reserved for the discipline of the boarding-school outing.

While the birth-rate for England and Wales fell from 34·2 (per thousand of the population) in 1880 to 28·7 in 1900 and 15·1 in 1938, its effect in slowing down the growth in population was in part offset by a simultaneous fall in the death-rate. For every thousand people living, fewer new ones were being born, but both these newcomers and those who had brought them into the world were, on the average, living appreciably longer than their forefathers, so that the number remaining alive at any one time continued to grow fairly rapidly. The decline in the death-rate was continuous, from 20·5 in 1880 to 18·2 in 1900, 12·4 in 1920, and 11·6 in 1938. The fall was due mainly to advances in medical knowledge and better hospital services, and perhaps also—especially in the twentieth century—to rather better feeding and housing. Put in terms of 'expectation of life', the improvement was spectacular. On the facts of life and death as England knew them around 1880, a baby safely born could expect not a psalmist's span of three score years and ten but only 43 years. In the England that went to war against Hitler, the statistical average was little short of the psalmist's span: 'expectation of life' of the new-born child was now 65 years, half as long again as the 43 of 1880. The change was a nation-wide change, though greatest in the industrial areas where death-rates had grimly reported how British workers missed the fresh air of the countryside. Some of the difference still remained: despite the great improvement (in Lancashire the death-rate was actually halved) Lancashire and Lanarkshire were still in the 'twenties, as they had been fifty years earlier, the counties with the highest death-rates.

The most striking element in this lengthening of human life, however, was the fall after 1900 in the infantile mortality rate. In 1880, three boys in every twenty and one girl in every eight did not complete one year of life; in 1900 the figures were actually a little worse. Thereafter, improvement was rapid and continuous, and by 1938 the risk of death within the first year had been almost halved since the beginning of the century. Girls continued to do better than boys (the infantile mortality rate in 1938 was 82 per thousand for boys and 66 for girls) but the boys' rate had had so far to fall that the doctors' success in saving babies was destined eventually to increase the proportion of men to women in the adult population.

The proportion of men to women has a bearing not only on a woman's chance of marriage but also on the proportion of workers to 'passengers' in the population; this proportion is affected not only by what is happening to boy and girl babies but also by what is happening to emigration and immigration. On the average, men and boys emigrate rather more than women and girls; and since, in most years, more people left Britain than came to it, this difference between the emigration-propensities of the sexes meant that Britain lost to other countries more males than females. The heavy emigration in the second half of the nineteenth century and the first years of the twentieth century therefore helped to create the 'surplus' of women which, aggravated by the slaughter in the First World War, numbered nearly 2 millions by 1930. From one decade to another migration out of and into the country could vary very substantially: in general, the more prosperous decades saw a high level of net emigration, while the depressed 1930s saw a net migration *into* Britain. This last feature emphasizes a motivation that became much more marked in this period: conditions in the country of *destination* rather than conditions in Britain itself seemed to matter most, though naturally a decline in opportunities at home did help to drive the young men away. The 'eighties, for example, were years of rapid development in most of the 'new' countries (the Americas and Australia, especially) and unusually large numbers were drawn to them from the depressed agricultural counties of England: net emigration in that decade exceeded 800,000. In the 'nineties there were longer spells of hesitation in the opening up of lands beyond the sea, while at home the farmers had in some measure learned to adapt themselves; consequently, though there were then more men of 'emigrating age', net emigration was a mere 120,000. The early 1900s saw a sharp increase: these were years of rapid development of the great dominions, and net emigration was almost on the scale of the 'eighties, despite the prosperity of leading British industries. After the wartime interruption, the outward flood was resumed, but it dried up at the end of the 1920s, and was actually reversed through most of the remaining years before the Second World War.

From the viewpoint of England's success in earning its living, it is important to remember that, whatever the broader effects of emigration, it did in detail often operate as a kind of safety-valve for pockets of population stranded in comparatively unwanted occupations and places. This is most frequently exemplified by the outflow of agricultural workers, especially from the corn-growing counties in the 1880s, but more narrowly localized examples can be found in spots where some traditional industry was being squeezed out of existence. Cornish mining (of tin and copper) went downhill rapidly in the 1870s, and during the next decade many of the younger men left the duchy to use their traditional skills in the new mines that were pulling the tentacles of settlement into remote corners of the new countries. Textile workers from midland and west-country centres, now losing ground to the manufacturers of the north, were also joining those farm labourers who felt that they must look for opportunity far away from home.

To the extent that the emigrants were going from relatively unwanted spots, the loss to Britain was less than when a brilliant engineer goes from a key post in an expanding industry. But it was still predominantly a loss of potential breadwinners who might have found useful employment in the home country: over the period 1871-1911, 42 per cent of the emigrants were males aged 18 to 30. The loss in a decade of half a million of the country's vigorous young men—and this was the scale in three decades out of five—could make a serious difference to the proportion of active workers to 'passengers' in the total population, especially when one of the other decades saw the decimation of similar age-groups in war. Proportions such as this—more generally, the structure or composition of the population—can have important influence on the standard of living of a people, quite independently of what is happening to the productive efficiency of the average worker. With every mouth God sends a pair of hands, but the mouth works much longer than the pair of hands, and there is no proverbial assurance that open mouths and active hands will keep in steady proportions. A falling birth-rate means a fall in the proportion of mouths to active hands, continuing for many years after it appears. For a falling death-rate there is no such simple rule: it depends upon the age-groups most affected. To the extent, for example, that the fall in these decades was at the infantile mortality end, it was as though more babies were born, and simply increased the proportion of children in the population. To the extent that it meant that women were living into their eighties, instead of dying in their sixties, the falling death-rate again meant an increasing proportion of 'passengers', though (unlike the greater survival of babies) there would in this case be no compensating rise in the vigorous teenagers and young married couples some years later. To the extent that the change was because doctors were saving active workers from industrial disease or other premature death (and this was at first the major element), the proportion of workers to passengers was raised—though later on there would be more pensioners to support.

Only by coincidental balancing of such conflicting factors could a population escape important changes in structure. In fact in these decades the changes already in process from earlier decades, and the large changes we have noted in birth- and death-rates and in migration within the period, ensured that the structure of the population changed appreciably at this time. The following Table summarizes the picture:

TABLE I

Age Composition of Population

(*Percentages*)

Age-groups	1881	1939
0–19	46	30
20–39	29	32
40–59	17	24
60 and over	7	13

[Source: *Papers of the Royal Commission on Population* (1950), vol. ii, p. 189.]

In a sense, this was an 'ageing' population—the average age in 1881 was 24, and in 1939 it was 32. If we look at the two 'ends', in 1939 there were many more old people (a high proportion of whom would not be full workers) but there were also far fewer children to be supported in every hundred of the population. Looking the other way round, and regarding the age-groups 20–59 as including most of the nation's working force, there were 46 of these among every 100 people in 1881, and 56 in every 100 in 1939. In effect, this was so many more pairs of hands to every 100 mouths: an important cause of the rise in the standard of living, even if the British people were choosing to take out some of their increased wealth in the shape of more schooldays for the fewer children.

Geographically, the increase in population was not quite evenly spread over England and Wales, and closer inspection reveals three major irregularities in the pattern. First, while any industry—even any large firm—that was growing fast, attracted people to its area and thus microscopically disturbed the geographical pattern of population, down to 1914 the attraction of coal-mining was on a uniquely huge scale. The coalfields, and especially those sharing in the export boom, had a high natural increase (coal-miners had big families and a surprisingly high survival rate) and they attracted migrants from neighbouring counties. Secondly, the swing of population northward, which had radically changed the economic and political balance of England during the eighteenth and nineteenth centuries, became less noticeable in the new century and was actually reversed in its second quarter. Thirdly, the concentration of population in a half-dozen conurbations continued, and among these Greater London was growing most of all. In these sprawling built-up areas—London, South-East Lancashire, Merseyside, West Midlands, West Yorkshire, and Tyneside—41 per cent of the population of England and Wales lived in 1911. By 1931, when the proportion in all the conurbations was still 41 per cent, more than half of these people were in Greater London. In the inter-war period some country towns near London took up the race: Chelmsford, Bedford, Luton, and Aylesbury were increasing their working populations faster than the fringe of London itself, and by 1939 nearly 30 per cent of England's population was in London and the Home Counties.

This swing of the population south-eastward was associated with the rise of new industries. It was also associated with the bicycle, the motor-car, the tram, the petrol bus, and better housing, and all these features helped to give a different character to the new urban developments. In 1939 a third of the houses in the country had been built in the last twenty years. In these new houses people lived more spaciously, and there were far fewer houses to the acre now that people could get more easily to work (and to the shops) by bicycle or bus. So the houses sprawled even further over the countryside: in the first four decades of the century, an area equal to the two counties of Buckingham and Bedford was newly covered by bricks and mortar. For market-gardening this was particularly

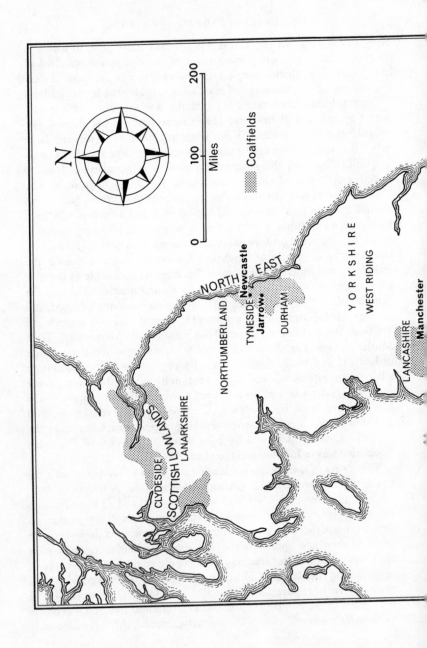

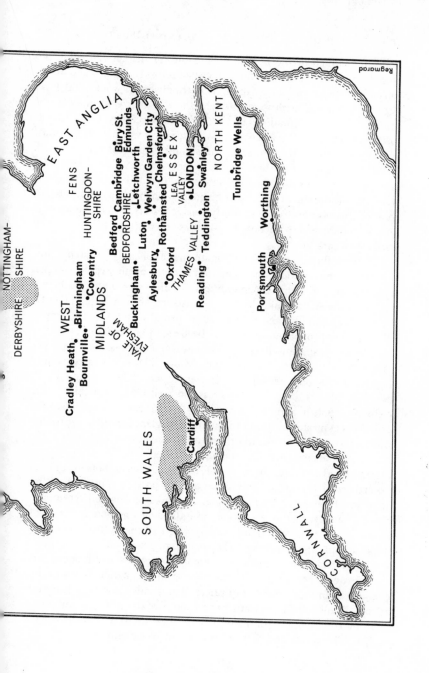

Regmarad

DERBYSHIRE · · · · NOTTINGHAM-SHIRE

EAST ANGLIA

FENS

HUNTINGDON-SHIRE

Bedford · Cambridge · Bury St. Edmunds
BEDFORDSHIRE
Luton · Letchworth
· Welwyn Garden City
Buckingham · Aylesbury · Rothamsted · Chelmsford
LEA ESSEX
· Oxford VALLEY
THAMES VALLEY · LONDON
Reading · Teddington · Swanley
NORTH KENT
Tunbridge Wells

Cradley Heath · Birmingham
Bournville · · Coventry
WEST
MIDLANDS
VALE OF EVESHAM

Portsmouth   Worthing

SOUTH WALES

Cardiff

CORNWALL

damaging: much of the land most suitable for market-gardening lies close to the towns, and as the houses pushed across the valleys and up the hillsides it began to look as though the Englishman would find fresh vegetables more difficult to get. Indeed there is some evidence that the growth of the conurbations in the nineteenth century had had unfortunate effects on the Englishman's diet, and it was not until canned vegetables came to the rescue in the second quarter of the twentieth century that this threat from the urban sprawl was evaded. There were other ways, too, in which the Englishman, more mobile than ever before, was changing the face of the land by his adaptation to urban life: England's coastline, barely spotted by the early seaside resorts, was filling up over long stretches, first with boarding-houses, then with bungalows, and finally with caravans.

The possibility of such escape from town life—a kind of existence now almost as characteristic of the south-east as of the north-west—was open to more and more Englishmen only because they now enjoyed a bigger margin of income beyond the bare subsistence of their forefathers. Of the 47 millions in England in 1939, as compared with the 30 millions in 1880, a bigger proportion were town-dwellers, by any criterion, but they could live more spacious lives because they could produce more for every man, woman, and child in the population. Through the remaining chapters of this book we shall be concerned with how, in some detail, they were able to secure this increase in well-being, for this is 'the economic problem' and economic history is concerned with man's varying success in mastering it. For the moment we glance ahead to the result: how, in measurable terms, did the wealth—the flow of income—of the English people change during these six decades?

Here we have to enter the prison of statistics. The components of total national production are so diverse that the only possible way of indicating the national income is by measuring the flow of goods and services in terms of money, just as we reckon an individual's income in terms of money. As with the individual, so also when all the individuals of the nation are grouped together, the money measure can be deceptive because of general movements in the purchasing power of money; it is therefore necessary to adjust the figures for 'money national income' by reference to an index number of prices. These index numbers cover up the logical difficulty in any attempt to compare the prices, at different dates, of combinations of items that change between one date and another. The goods and services that could be bought for a hundred pounds were different in relative importance, different in quality, even different in their essential nature in 1939 from what they were in 1880. Motor-cycles and radio sets did not exist in 1880, nor were such common and important articles as bread and clothing at all the same at these extreme dates of our period. So when they use index numbers to adjust money figures, economists are to some extent riding roughshod over the real changes that make our economic history. The longer the period, the more damaging is this flaw in the process of adjustment by index number; over six decades—especially decades when the majority of the population had little margin above the physical subsistence requirements—the damage is perhaps just tolerable. Squeezing the infinite variety of goods and services into the statistical prison, economic statisticians[1] have produced the figures which show, in Table 2, the total national income and the average income per head, in terms of money of theoretically constant value. (The figures are for the *United Kingdom*; there are no separate figures for England and Wales. The value-of-money adjustment has been made by using cost-of-living index numbers to convert all figures into pounds of the value ruling in 1900.)

TABLE 2

Net National Income of the United Kingdom (1900 prices)

	Total (£mill.)	Per head (£)
1880	932	26·9
1899	1,799	44·1
1913	2,021	44·3
1925	2,070	45·9
1938	2,725	57·4

The intermediate years shown in this Table have been selected as approximate turning-points in the behaviour of complete annual series. Between 1880 and 1899 (which was a boom year) national income almost doubled, implying an increase of income per head of over 60 per cent. Then the pace changed sharply: in the remaining years before the First World War, the increase was scarcely more than sufficient to keep pace with the continuing rise in the number of heads. Then there were the war years, and violent fluctuation in the immediate post-war period,

[1] C. H. Feinstein (for 1880, 1899, and 1913), and A. R. Prest (for 1925 and 1938), as shown on pp. 367-8 of Mitchell and Deane, *Abstract of British Historical Statistics*.

until in the middle 'twenties total income and income per head settled down at levels not much above the pre-war level. In the later 'twenties the rise was resumed; in fourteen years about 25 per cent was added to income per head. In the last years before the Second World War, the 'real' national income totalled nearly three times the 1880 level, representing rather more than twice as much per head as in 1880. The crucial interest for human welfare is, of course, in the per-head figures; and these are worth summarizing once more. For what such figures spread over sixty years are worth, we can say that man's success in solving his economic problem was rather more than doubled, and that nearly all this improvement came in two great bursts, 1880-99 and 1926-36.

It is perhaps surprising that so large a part of the improvement should have been concentrated in these two spells totalling only half of the sixty years of our period. Yet a complete annual series would show that the improvement was confined to as few as twenty of the sixty years, for the two long spells included many years of backsliding or stagnation in the level of real income. What were the causes of these irregularities that were big enough to make an impression on national totals? The answer to this question must be a large part of the economic history of the English people in this period. In Chapters 2, 3, and 4 we shall seek something of an answer, by inquiring first (in Chapter 2) into the success of the Englishman in getting what he needs by exchanging his products with those of other countries, and then (in Chapters 3 and 4) more specifically into the short-term fluctuations that show their mark in nearly every index of economic activity. After these chapters we leave these broad themes, and proceed to inquire (in Chapters 5, 6, and 7) into Englishmen's experience in some of those particular groups of activities we call 'industries' or 'trades'. In Chapters 8 and 9 we return to more general inquiries: in 8, to the conditions of work and the efforts of society to lessen hardships; in 9, to the supply and organization of the capital that aids the productive processes. Finally, in Chapter 10 we outline, without answering them, some of the questions that have been left unanswered though they would have to be answered if an account of the economic struggle were fully to satisfy our curiosity.

2
The Export Trade

ONE OF THE MOST REMARKABLE MOVEMENTS in economic history has had its full share of emphasis from the historians: this is the revolution in industrial and agricultural techniques in eighteenth-century England, which made possible the sustenance, probably on a slowly rising standard, of the surge of population in the latter part of that century. At least as impressive, however, was the surge of production in the middle third of the nineteenth century, associated with the refinement and generalization of the previous technical changes, and particularly with the exploitation of steam power in transport by land and by sea. It was this second phase that allowed, for the first time, a clear and substantial rise in the material standard of living, despite the high rate at which the population continued to grow. But the technical changes were not by themselves sufficient to provide for this rise in total consumption: it was necessary in addition that Britain's foreign trade should grow fast. It was, in short, by becoming 'the workshop of the world' that Britain achieved this impressive increase in wealth. This development left the standard of living of Britain's 30 million people extraordinarily dependent on the success of Britain's export trade. In a rough-and-ready way one can say that around 1880 the British economy was geared to the ability to sell to the outside world the output of one worker in every five. What could happen to the standard of living in the succeeding period— the decades with which we are immediately concerned—therefore depended in quite large part on the readiness of the outside world to continue to buy British produce on this scale. The experience of Britain's export trade is therefore the key to much else that happened in the decades after 1880.

Under Giffen's persuasion the British people had learned to take note

of overseas trade figures, and the totals for the export trade showed no
cause for alarm until after the 1914 war. From £223 M. in 1880 their total
value had risen to £233 M. in 1899, despite rather lower prices, and then
well beyond £500 M. in 1913, seemingly giving the lie to those who
argued that industrialization elsewhere was sounding the death-knell of
British prosperity. After a bumper spell in 1919-20, the figures ranged
between £700 M. and £800 M. in the 'twenties, but after wartime inflation pounds meant much less, and these figures of total values implied
quantities disappointing in relation to the immediately pre-war experience. For a long time, however, it was possible to believe that the difficulties of the export trades were substantially the aftermath of war, and
it was only when both values and quantities dwindled in the 'thirties that
more fundamental causes were universally admitted. Industrialization
in other countries had after all undermined Britain's export trade, and
it was the extreme prosperity of the last years before the war that now
looked paradoxical.

In fact the same fundamental causes were operating throughout the
period, and neither the Jeremiahs who pointed to the new foreign competition nor those who had pointed to the continuing growth (till 1914)
of total trade were seeing the impact of world development as an impact
of conflicting forces on British export possibilities. These conflicting
forces—with the balance swinging now this way, now that—were at work
all the time, and their effects can be perceived in the composition of trade
long before 1914, whether we analyse by markets or by commodities. To
avoid the oddities of particular years, we shall look, in Table 3, at groups
of years, all in periods of peace.

The figures in Table 3 are absolute figures of values: in interpreting
them, we have to remember that wholesale prices, not very different
between the first and second periods, were 70-80 per cent higher in
1922-5 than they had been before the war, and that they fell a little, but
not back to pre-war levels, between 1922-5 and 1935-8. When allowance
has been made for this price distortion, the apparent rise in total values
between pre-war and post-war disappears. In particular, the *real* decline
of British exports to the U.S.A., following pre-war stagnation, becomes
almost a collapse, and the post-war collapse of the Indian market can be
seen as a decline that more than wiped out the moderate pre-war expansion. In Western Europe also—an area that had been of leading importance in Britain's 'workshop' period—the growth had been relatively slow
in the pre-war period and was more than wiped out in the years between

the wars. Broadly, Britain was losing her best customers, first in the U.S.A. and then in India and Western Europe. In the rest of the Americas and Asia (where Japan suddenly became important) British exporters gained fast before the war, but lost even faster after it. Only in the new African markets did any compensatory growth continue.

TABLE 3

Destinations of U.K. Exports

In millions of £, four-year periods

TOTAL	1880–3 940	1909–12 1,750	1922–5 3,060	1935–8 1,860
By destinations				
Western Europe	134	205	414	177
Rest of Europe and other Mediterranean countries	229	481	693	469
Rest of Africa	38	132	226	250
U.S.A.	119	119	221	102
British North America	35	82	113	99
Central and S. America	81	196	254	143
India	121	199	355	142
Rest of Asia	70	155	303	129

[Source: Summarized from Table 12 in Chapter XI of Mitchell and Deane, *Abstract of British Historical Statistics*.]

This changing regional pattern cannot be ascribed to any single cause, but equally it is not just a jumble of unrelated movements. The clue is to be found by seeing what was happening in the outside world not simply as a rise of competitive industries but as rapid economic growth of which industrialization was but one aspect. It is by disentangling varied aspects of economic growth, and not just one among them, that we can perceive the major sources of change in the pattern of Britain's export trade. Among these influences, implicit in the process of growth, were changes in technical methods of production, and differing rates of change in different commodities could alter the flow of trade in particular commodities. To some of these special *commodity* aspects of the flow of trade, as they affected Britain, we shall return; but first there are two broader aspects of economic growth to claim attention. For the history of the export trade reflects the twofold nature of the development of the outside world: the growth of total demand (the *complementarity* aspect) and the growth of alternative supplies (the *competitive* aspect).

Growth meant that the various countries of the world were increasing their production and therefore their incomes. They were achieving this partly by borrowing from British and other sources and using the borrowed money to spend on equipment and consumption goods, but also by increasing their populations and applying both new and old techniques to the opening up of natural resources. Both their spending on development and their spending on a rising standard of consumption (as their productivity rose) implied increasing demands for imported goods. The increasing demand for imports into developing countries was a force helping exporters from other countries, including Britain. This aspect of economic growth is called the *complementarity* aspect, for growth in one country gave direct stimulus to growth in others. It did not mean help to Britain alone, for Britain was not the only country that could produce goods wanted in the developing countries; but there was a bigger world market in which British exporters could seek a share. If a country was developing rapidly because Britain had begun buying food and raw materials from it, or because Britain was lending to it, the expansion of the market was not, it must be emphasized, one in which British exporters alone could benefit, for trading facilities were on the whole *multilateral*. Payments in foreign trade had long been multilateral, through the development of foreign exchange markets, allowing a country that was earning pounds (by selling to Britain) to use those pounds to buy other currencies to pay for goods from any country in the world. The constraints of shipping still, even today, enforce some link between import and export trades in bulky materials, but the rapid manœuvrability of ships in the late nineteenth century had already made this link a loose one. British lending, it is true, did sometimes carry some differential advantage for British exporters; but in the main the impulse of expanding markets was an impulse to all-comers. It was an impulse emanating not by any means only from the 'new' countries of the other continents: Western and Central Europe was also growing fast and its increasing wealth made it an expanding market for British goods, even though conflicting forces were slowing this expansion down.

The most fundamental of these conflicting forces was the other aspect, the *competitive* aspect, of economic growth; it was of this that the Jeremiahs, haunted by American bustle and 'Made in Germany' labels, were most keenly aware. As other countries developed, they became more able to supply themselves with goods they wanted and had hitherto imported. Then, 'catching-up' in industrial development, they could go one step further, and appear as competitors of Britain in Britain's other markets. Finally they could even appear as competitors in Britain's home market. This competitive aspect of economic development became of great importance in world markets in the latter part of the nineteenth century. In so far as Britain's export capacity depended on a lead in technical knowledge and in highly skilled labour, it could not be expected to last. Britain had never had any monopoly of either craftsmen or technical inventiveness, and the emigration of skilled men—a large movement in the 'workshop period' in the mid-nineteenth century—had increased the speed at which manufacturing industries elsewhere could become competitive with the British. In terms of the markets for British exports, this rising competition showed itself in two ways: in a widening circle of markets British exporters found themselves undercut by domestic manufacturers, and in the less developed countries, though the total market might be growing fast, British exporters faced new competition from European and American manufacturers.

What was happening to British exports in any particular market depended mainly on the relative strengths of these conflicting forces. If the complementarity aspect was very strong, as in a fast-growing country with a special taste for British goods, British exports would soar. But if the competition aspect was strong, while the complementarity aspect was weak—if the country was not growing so fast but was copying Britain's industrial techniques—British export trade to that country would tend to stagnate and might soon be damaged in other markets as well. In different regions of the world the balance between complementarity and competitiveness changed at different times, and so the distribution of British exports between countries changed. It seems likely that in the long run technical differences between countries become less, so that there is an underlying tendency for the balance in any one market to swing, with development, towards greater competitiveness. This tendency was operating before, throughout, and after our period; but the balance was not changing in quite the same way everywhere at once, and the total of British exports could therefore go on rising long after particular markets had begun to show that competitiveness was catching up on complementarity.

Not that complementarity ever became a spent force. Indeed, one of the most remarkable features of Britain's trade right down to 1914 was the continued rise of exports to Western and Central Europe. In terms of the *rate of increase*, Europe was one of Britain's less healthy markets, but even a slow rate of increase in a big market (as Europe had long been) meant quite a useful increase in absolute terms. In fact, Europe was growing so fast that despite her relatively advanced industrialization and the competitiveness this implied, the influence of complementarity still prevailed, and right down to 1914 the growth of European wealth remained a stimulant, on balance, to British export trade and so to Britain's own prosperity. When the 1914 war and its aftermath interrupted Europe's economic growth, this was a large part of the explanation of the failure of the British economy to grow fast enough to afford a further rise in the living standard of its population. In the United States market, a market on which the British export trade had thriven so spectacularly through much of the nineteenth century, the balance swung more abruptly to the competitive side. The tremendous burst of activity in the U.S.A. after the Civil War provided—by its appetite for British exports—a major thrust in the British boom, but it was the last thrust of its kind. After 1880 the U.S.A. continued to develop rapidly— and as irregularly as ever—but it was much more self-sufficient, and it was buying relatively more from Britain's competitors. The pattern of this history of Anglo-American trade was to be repeated in other directions, perhaps most abruptly in Japan. The economic development of Japan on modern lines began only after 1868; then until 1914 Japan was a fast-growing outlet for a wide range of British manufactures. Before 1914 British traders there already faced stiff competition from other foreigners, but total imports were growing so rapidly that Britain's share was rising in absolute terms, quite sharply. The European war, however, gave Japanese manufacturers—especially in textiles—a chance they were fully ready to take, and the extraordinary growth of Japan after 1920 gave no further scope for British exports. In the 'thirties, indeed, Japanese manufactures invaded other countries on a huge scale, and finally knocked at the doors of Lancashire itself.

The same sort of movement—rapid growth of imports from Britain, then the appearance of European competitors, then a surge of domestic competition, and finally the outbreak of the domestic manufacturers into world markets—happened more slowly in India. There it mattered a great deal because India had been such a large market for Britain: in the early 'eighties as important as the U.S.A. and almost as important as all the Western European countries put together. The growth in Britain's trade to India continued to be fairly rapid until 1920; thereafter British exporters struggled to maintain their share, and finally had to acknowledge defeat in the years before the Second World War, when India emerged as a competitor *outside India*. In Latin America something like the same process appeared. This was a rapidly developing market before 1914, though one in which Britain faced strong competition from other countries. In the inter-war period this competition increased in strength, but domestic competition was slow to develop and did not reach the ultimate phase of competition in world markets. Only in African markets did the trends favourable to Britain continue to predominate right through the period. Apart from Egypt and the other North African countries which, in terms of economic development, formed part of a Mediterranean area unlike the typically 'colonial' territories, African markets for British goods grew rapidly right through the period. There was European and later American competition in these African markets, but the opportunities were new enough for total growth to be rapid, and competitive domestic production appeared only much later in the twentieth century.

The changes in trade in particular commodities, or classes of commodities, show this same combination and balancing of forces operating on Britain's power to sell in the outside world. The period 1880-1940 covers the second and third phase of the railway age: though railway construction was almost over in Britain itself, it continued on a huge scale in much of the outside world until 1914, and even after that the replacement demand for the world's railways remained a large element in international trade. But what this all meant for Britain's iron and steel industry was not what it had been before 1880. Almost all the rails required for the construction of U.S.A. railways had, in the middle decades of the century, gone from Britain, but this was never true after 1880. The Americans continued for decades to construct thousands of miles of new line every year, but in the face of European and domestic competition British sales of rails and other equipment dwindled, although British investors continued to provide much of the money. In the twentieth century the U.S.A. became substantially self-sufficient in railway material, besides taking most of the market provided by Canada's new railway mileage, and competing seriously with the British product in South America, South Africa, and Australia. In the early days of South American railway construction, authorities used to reckon that a third or even half of the capital was spent on goods imported from Britain, but before 1914 the Germans as well as the Americans were pushing into the market, knocking down the British share. Not that this was happening everywhere at once: India, for example, continued to draw mainly on the British iron and steel industry, far into the new century.

In other directions, too, the total export earnings were being significantly affected by what was happening to the trade in individual commodities. Some of the most instructive changes can be perceived in the following Table: the figures are for single years unaffected by war.

TABLE 4

U.K. Exports of Commodities

(millions of £)

Year	Total	Coal	Iron and steel	Machinery	Cotton goods	Chemicals	Vehicles and aircraft	Electrical goods
1880	223	8·4	27·2	9·3	75·6	8·8	*	*
1900	291	38·6	31·6	19·6	69·8	13·1	0·3	3·3
1913	525	53·7	55·4	37·0	127·2	22·0	5·4	5·4
1930	570	49·2	51·3	52·0	87·6	23·4	17·9	11·9
1938	470	40·7	42·9	60·7	49·7	22·1	24·7	13·4

* Not separately classified; negligible at this date.

[Source: Table 8 in Chapter XI of Mitchell and Deane, *Abstract of British Historical Statistics.*]

As with the figures appearing earlier in this chapter, it is important to remember that there were big swings in the general level of prices. There was a fall, of the order of 20 per cent, between 1880 and 1900, then a rise (20-25 per cent) to 1913, and a sharp rise (60 per cent) has to be allowed for when comparing both 1930 and 1938 with 1913.

Three features stand out beyond all others in this Table: the declining relative importance of iron and steel and, more sharply, of cotton goods; the upsurge of the 'new' exports—machinery, chemicals, vehicles, aircraft, and electrical goods; and the rise and fall of coal, a story all its own.

Iron and steel exports were still rising until 1913; we have already seen this as a commodity group in which the complementarity aspect and the competitive aspect were both very important in this period. Miles of new railways all over the world and many other features of economic development were adding to the world's appetite for iron and steel (more iron at first, more steel later) and to the world's ability to pay for them. But in this swelling market Britain was meeting altogether more powerful competition as the iron mines of America and Europe, and the furnaces built around them, were developed. After the war the competitive force proved the stronger and total values, even at post-war prices, fell below the 1913 level. In cotton goods the corresponding movement was even more decided. The huge figures of Britain's exports of cotton goods right through the nineteenth century bred a mentality to which failure seemed unbelievable, but in the detailed facts the writing was on the wall for all to read, long before 1914. In the last decade of peace the total figure had gone up by a jump big even by the standards of nineteenth-century expansion, but this growth in the total was more than due to expansion in more distant markets, obscuring the decline in the older markets where competition from European exporters or from domestic manufacturers was pushing the English traders out. For too long the books told generations of English schoolchildren that Lancashire had unique advantages for the cotton industry: the truth is rather that cotton processing has been one of the easiest branches of industry to establish in a great variety of countries. In one country after another the first step in industrialization was the building of cotton mills. This was happening long before 1914; competitiveness was on the tail of complementarity and wartime disruption of trade only hastened a process that was bound to lead sooner or later to an absolute decline in the amount of the British product wanted by the outside world. Instead, the rather gradual development of European manufactures before 1914 was but a thin foreshadowing of what was to happen in world textile production when the abundant Asiatic labour supplies were drafted into cotton mills first in Japan, then in India and China.

Coal was another commodity in which change was very rapid and—because Britain had a start in the export of coal and was able easily to increase its output—the change was peculiarly important to Britain. World economic development before 1914 was almost exclusively on the basis that the energy used to supplement manual labour was obtained by burning coal. New railways meant more locomotives burning coal, and new steamships, replacing sailing-ships, meant more coal-burners belching smoke over the oceans of the world. Iron and steel and other metals were needed in ever-increasing tonnages, and smelting and manufacture involved the burning of coal. When so much of the technique of the railway and steamship age was still quite novel, and British seaboard coal was abundant, the use of coal remained fantastically extravagant by the standards of later technique. So the world's consumption of coal went on rising by a regular 4 per cent a year right down to 1913; and Britain had no difficulty—with abundant labour supply for the pick-and-shovel industry it then was—in securing the lion's share of the market. In 1880, out of 147 million tons mined in the United Kingdom, 18 million tons went to the outside world, and in 1913, of 287 million tons mined, 98 millions were exported. Quite apart from the values in question (10 per cent of the total value of United Kingdom exports in 1913), the movement of these huge tonnages helped to shape the world's shipping, just as the tonnages moving inside the country influenced the shape and the habits of the railways. These were the decades when hundreds of acres of new docks were constructed in South Wales and elsewhere to handle this bulky export trade: Cardiff almost overnight became one of the most prosperous cities of the world and her civic buildings stand today a monument of the architecture of the Age of Coal.

Cardiff's civic pride and its vast acreage of docks have long outlived coal's heyday. In the middle 1920s the tonnage of British coal exported went below 70 millions, and in the last years before the Second World War 50 millions was the general level. The 'twenties heard—as for other failures—endless excuses of temporary disturbance: the disorganization of European trade, the withdrawal of Russia from the world economy, the overpricing of British coal by the ill-starred return to the gold standard in 1925. Certainly there were temporary factors at work, but they blinded people to the fundamental change that had come over the world trade in coal: against the 4 per cent pre-war, world consumption of coal was now increasing by only 0·3 per cent a year, to a small extent because people were using other sources of energy, but mainly because they were not sending so much coal unused up the chimney stack. Long before 1914 there were prophetic signs: even before 1900 the energy was being obtained and used more economically by the generation of electricity, and battleships were burning oil. The change was world-wide, and the depression of the coal trade was an international depression; but Britain had been a chief source in the long coal boom, and its ultimate failure hit Britain hard.

Towards the end of the nineteenth century, and much more vociferously in the first third of the twentieth, industrialists complained that Protectionist tariffs were crippling trade, and especially the relative chances of British exports. There was substance in the charge, though less than a listener might have been led to suppose. By the middle of the nineteenth century the Free Trade presumption of English classical economics had its maximum effect on fiscal policies all over the world. This did not mean that every country had followed England in abjuring import duties for protection of its industries; but from 1860 the remaining hindrances of this kind gave English exporters no headaches. Then new stars appeared in the economists' firmament: Vienna began its long eminence in economic doctrine and, partly under Vienna's influence and partly infused with the new German nationalism, Protectionism entered on a new lease of life as a policy for economic growth. In 1879, as part of an industrialization policy, the new German Empire adopted a seriously Protectionist tariff of import duties. Italy had already, in 1878, adopted a moderate measure of the same kind, and followed this up with an altogether steeper tariff in 1887. France, which Gladstone and Cobden had won for freer trade in 1860, recanted in 1882. In the United States, where the 'new industry argument' for Protectionism always had a strong hold, there was a new tariff in 1883 and then, in 1890, the high tariff to which McKinley's name was at once attached. These were only beginnings: thenceforward the world tide was strongly Protectionist right through until, in reaction against the extremities of the 1930s, ideals of multilateral trade swung back into fashion in the reconstruction phase at the end of the Second World War. (Britain herself at first resisted the Protectionist tide, but eventually joined in a small way with a Safeguarding of Industries Act in 1921, followed by further measures in 1925 and 1932.)

The effects of foreign tariffs on British export trade varied greatly from one industry to another. Sometimes the impact was direct and severe: the tinplate trade, so important to South Wales, was knocked hard in the 1890s by American import duties, and soda ash suffered by the German tariff in 1879.[1] Against the total picture of British trade, these were small items but, because the hurt was concentrated and so obviously due to the foreign tariffs, their effect on opinion was out of all proportion. Bigger industries had their troubles too. The German and American iron and steel industries were helped to their feet by tariff protection, but no sooner were the import duties established than they became insignificant, because the advantages these countries enjoyed in their own mineral resources came fully into play and made their industries

[1] Soda ash is an important material of the soap, glass, and chemical industries.

competitive, not only in their own markets but in other countries as well. So tariffs, in the event, made little difference in this trade, but the success of the Germans and Americans, so soon after they had received tariff encouragement, helped to give vogue to tariff policies for industrialization.

In textiles, the effects were mixed. Local cotton industries often secured some recognition by tariff-minded ministers—as in the U.S.A. in 1883, for example—but in this earlier period the duties were mainly on the cheaper classes of cotton goods (which were the first to be manufactured when the industry found a new home) and do not seem to have greatly hurt Lancashire, always more active in the finer end of the trade. Occasionally, tariff increases positively helped cotton, as when high duties on woollen goods in the McKinley tariff persuaded Americans to wear more cotton and less woollens. The woollen industry was thus doubly caught; indeed, among the major industries it was hurt most of all. All the major countries raised tariff walls against it, and this at a time when fashion, decreeing fewer flannel petticoats and (eventually) shorter skirts, was working against the industry. Lancashire was able, too, to escape the consequences of high tariffs in the temperate countries by pushing sales into new markets in tropical Asia and Africa. Naturally enough, hot countries were not so obliging for the woollen manufacturers of Yorkshire, though a section of the industry elsewhere—blankets at Witney—throve as never before on new markets among the black races of Africa.

Britain—and British economic thought—at first held back the spread of Protectionism in Empire markets, but the Canadians were already in 1879 exercising their autonomy in fiscal policy, and in the new century the self-governing Dominions were swimming vigorously with the Protectionist tide. For much longer—until 1917—Britain was able politically to hold India to Free Trade; it was an important exception. For longer still, the newer tropical colonies in Africa and elsewhere were held to the British Free Trade tradition. This difference between Empire markets and the high-tariff markets of the European and American nations certainly helped to swing the direction of trade. This swing—Empire markets becoming more important in the total—was big enough to excite notice before 1914, and it became stronger afterwards. In the middle of the nineteenth century about 30 per cent of British exports had gone to the Empire; before 1914 this had crept up to 35, and in the 1930s to 43. Of textiles and iron and steel goods the proportions had been rather larger than this, but more striking still was the fact that in some of the newer export trades—in motor-cars, soap, and books—the proportions going to Empire markets were very high indeed. This rising relative importance of Empire trade (it showed on the import side too) helped to give an imperialist slant to the 'Tariff Reform' movement that was gathering strength over the turn of the century. It chimed in well with the political enthusiasm for Empire, the effervescence of which showed in the celebrations of the Queen's two jubilees in 1887 and 1897. Imperial Preference—lower duties on imports from the Empire than on those from other sources—was introduced in 1919. For a time its main expression was in the 'revenue' duties (so favouring Indian and Ceylon teas against those of China), but it became much more important after the Ottawa Conference in 1932. By that time, however, overseas trade had become, on the face of it, much less important to Britain: in relation to National Income, overseas trade in the 1930s had only half the value it had had through the half-century before 1914. Indeed, it was partly in an effort to save in Empire markets something of what had been lost elsewhere that Britain turned imperially Protectionist.

The underlying trends that were to limit so severely Britain's power to earn a living in the 1930s were thus already at work half a century earlier. Above all, competition from other people was always pressing into new directions as other countries developed, although at first the stronger force was the expansion of markets that development equally meant. In the last twenty years under Victoria, Britain's success in maintaining and expanding exports brought rich returns in the standard of living, for each pound's worth of exports was bringing much more in victuals than ever before, thanks to the new continental railways and more efficient shipping that brought food and raw materials from distant lands. After that, though the remaining years to 1914 were years of extraordinarily rapid growth in the world and of fantastic growth of British exports, the struggle was in some ways more difficult and it was certainly disappointing in its rewards for the ordinary Englishman. An unusually high proportion of the proceeds of exports went, in these years, to finance new investments abroad and these investments, though of great importance to the economic development of the world (and so of some help to the export markets), brought little immediate return. Moreover, the spasm of rapid cheapening of goods as the ships landed them in British ports was over: on the whole, the 'terms of trade'—the yield in imports of each pound's worth of exports—were turning against Britain.

B

Then came the upset of the First World War and its aftermath, and when the world at last recovered its wealth—in the middle 'twenties—it was a world that had gained in competitiveness and it was a more Protectionist world. The process of adjustment Britain had to make was grossly underrated and little progress had been made in regenerating export capacity when the world slump overwhelmed everybody in 1929–32. In the 'thirties world recovery was never complete. Looking over the whole post-1914 period, the competitive effects of world development were more powerful than any stimulus Britain received from the limping and discontinuous growth of world consumption. When, after 1950, the world learned again how to get rich quickly, Britain's export trade showed that competitive forces could be held at bay sufficiently for Britain to feel the benefit of the world's enrichment. In this new phase the great surge of British exports was to be mainly from a new group of industries;[1] of this there had been prophetic signs in the new exports, especially to Empire countries, in the 'thirties, but their witness had been obscured in the general gloom of a stagnant world.

Within these longer phases in the development of Britain's export business there were shorter ups and downs that were important both directly for Britain's livelihood and in influencing the trends of thought that lay behind the re-shaping of economic policy. These fluctuations fitted fairly closely the general fluctuations in the country's income, emphasizing the dependence of British workmen on what could be sold to overseas markets. Before 1914, the worst years were in the middle 'eighties, the middle 'nineties, 1901–2, and 1908–9; the best were 1882, 1890, 1900, 1907, and 1913. These were reflections of the general movement of trade over the greater part of the world, and this was not quite what had been happening before 1875. Through the middle decades of the nineteenth century Britain's export trade had found its tune called by the activity of business in the U.S.A.: when Uncle Sam had a burst of economic development, British exports jumped up and business activity inside Britain followed suit. In the last quarter of the century, and down to 1914, the U.S.A. remained important to Britain, but it was a world trade-cycle rather than an American trade-cycle that Britain followed. The part played in this by Britain's own overseas lending—which had always been an important factor in the American fluctuations—was not simple. There was certainly still some association between British lending and the pace at which the outside world would buy

[1] See Chap. 5.

British goods: economic development of the Argentine, Australia, and Canada had decided influence, and these countries were drawing on British capital. What was happening in Continental Europe, however, was also of great importance to British exporters, and this had little or no connexion with British overseas lending.

The immediately post-war boom and slump, covering only 1919-22, was a world-wide phenomenon that carried Britain's export trade up and then abruptly down with it. After that, however, the business activity of countries lost its world-wide pattern; the 'twenties especially present a confused picture in which different countries were recovering from the upheaval of 1914-20 in different ways and at very different rates. The British export record was distorted by the prolonged coal strikes of 1921 and 1926, and the later 'twenties saw no real recovery, 1929 standing out not as a true peak year but as the year before the great collapse. Then the world-wide pattern of slump, recovery, and recession reasserted itself, but with the United States again coming to dominate the scene. The bottom was reached in 1932-3; the slow recovery that followed took the level of exports to a 1937 peak that was still a long way below the plateau of the late 'twenties. It was a recovery, in fact, that appeared to be interrupted in 1938 before it had spent itself in the old way, and the word 'Stagnation' crept into economic literature. The depression of the outside world, partly because it had been so deep and so prolonged, had been unusual in its effects on the British economy: Britain, like other countries, had in some slight degree learned before 1940 to live rather more on herself, rather less on trade with others. Because Britain had in so high degree geared her living, in the previous century, to her power to earn in the outside world, this was an inescapably painful adjustment, and in no sense was it complete when the Second World War forced a completely new turn of the rudder.

3
The Trade Cycle, 1880–1914

THE ECONOMIC HISTORIAN is concerned with man's varying success in extracting, from the resources at his command, the flow of goods and services on which he can live: more strictly, from which he can live today and make some provision for tomorrow. As already noted, during these sixty years real income per head rather more than doubled; but this increase came irregularly. Most of it came in twenty of the sixty years, and there were, interrupting these periods of increasing income, years when the economy was stagnant or even declining. The fact that there were these irregularities—these economic fluctuations—was of great importance in the life of the nation through these decades, and this chapter and the next are therefore devoted to an account and some explanation of these fluctuations and what they meant in practical terms to the English people.

A cursory examination of the figures of national income year by year, in relation to the more prominent events, at once suggests that the irregularities in the growth of income may be broadly ascribed to sources of four quite different kinds:

1. Technical progress—the increase in man's knowledge of how to manipulate the physical world to satisfy his needs—does not occur smoothly. Invention comes spasmodically, and so does the more directly relevant process of applying the new ideas in production on an industrial scale. There is an everlasting stream of invention, but the stream runs sometimes more strongly, sometimes less, and particularly there is bunching in the widespread application of new techniques. Some of the more important of these technical changes are discussed in later chapters; it will be seen that, though England experienced no such widespread transformation as had followed the exploitation of steam-power in the

previous century, there were changes amounting to technical revolutions in some important lines of activity. The bunching of these changes over the time-span was itself sufficient to prevent growth from consisting of a single smooth upward sweep.

2. The terms of external trade fluctuated. One-fifth or more of the nation's energies went into the production of goods and services to sell overseas, because Englishmen wanted products of other countries as well as those of their own country. As explained in Chapter 2, success in these efforts depended on a balancing of competitiveness and complementarity with change in the outside world, and the balance swung now this way, now that. When—as in the closing decades of the nineteenth century, and again in 1925-35—the productivity of the outside world was going ahead faster in terms of the things Britain wanted than in terms of the things Britain could make, every pound's worth of exports brought a bigger return in imports: the terms of trade swung in Britain's favour. At other times—and this was important in 1900-14—the terms of trade swung against Britain, and the standard of living in Britain practically ceased to rise, despite the continuance of technical progress in British industry. The effects of these long swings in the terms of trade seem to have been the major cause of the broader irregularities in the growth of real income over these sixty years.

3. The war of 1914-18 had effects that are obvious enough, in that people who might have been occupied in producing consumable goods (or capital goods for adding to future production) were diverted to the armed forces or to making munitions and other materials of war. In addition, there was the loss of productivity immediately due to dislocation. Thus there was during the years 1914-18 an actual fall in the flow of real income (excluding from 'income' the products that were shot away on the battlefield). After the war there was quick recovery, but it was anything but steady: first there was a minor slump, then a fantastic burst of recovery, then a long phase of low-income years followed by irregular growth in the middle 'twenties; much of this post-war irregularity had its roots in the wartime dislocation of the smooth progress of the economy. For nearly a quarter of our sixty years, that is to say, the growth of income suffered special irregularities having their roots in the war of 1914-18. All the more normal causes of fluctuation were still more or less operative, but superimposed was the deep and prolonged disturbance of normal economic life by the tremendous economic effort of war.

4. Finally, the period was marked—obviously and uncomfortably for the people who lived through it—by variations in the degree to which the productive resources (of land, labour, capital, and enterprise) were employed. These fluctuations in the *degree of activity* were astonishingly regular, occurring in fairly long cycles, one cycle following another in regular sequence, broken only by the war. Because of their regularity, and because observers came to believe that the boom bore within itself the seeds of the following slump, and the slump itself engendered succeeding boom, the phenomenon was labelled 'the trade cycle'. It was a phenomenon that had been visible since the eighteenth century, but in its regularity and importance it was characteristic rather of the nineteenth century, and it is certainly one of the most important features of the British economy in the sixty years before 1939. When, taking our eyes off the broad sweep of decades, we fasten on any particular peacetime year, and want to know how successful Englishmen were in earning a living in that year, the first question arising is, how did that year stand in the trade cycle?

The trade cycle was so very important for three reasons: its effect on national production and so on the average standard of living that could be enjoyed; its effect on the employment of people—or rather on their unemployment—and so on their poverty and unhappiness; and its effect on economic and political thought. There were other aspects of significance, notably the distortions of the general level of prices, which were all part of the story and carried their own disadvantages into the ordinary life of the people; but the hard core of the problem of the trade cycle was the periodic waste of labour and other resources that stood idle during the phase of depression. It was this periodic unemployment of resources that allowed national income to fall, and it was this unemployment that was one of the principal causes of poverty and misery. At a time when the social conscience was developing an altogether new sensitiveness to the problems of poverty, the trade cycle became a major intellectual challenge: its existence coloured the approach to a wide range of problems of economic policy. The cycle's persistence throughout the period prompted new questions for theoretical economists, eventually giving a new slant to the science of economics and—after 1939—provoking a revolution in public finance.

Though there was a concomitant cycle in prices, the cycle was most prominently a cycle in *activity*. Thinking of it in this way, in isolation from the changes in technical productivity, the terms of trade, and the general level of prices (which is related to other factors as well as the trade cycle), it is best to leave aside the figures for money income or real income, and to abstract as best we can from the underlying upward trend in production. The phenomenon is shown most clearly in the index of 'industrial activity' prepared by W. H. Beveridge and J. H. Wilson.[1] This index is a statistician's device, not measuring the actual volume of output, employment, or the like from year to year, but using such statistics to show, without distraction, how activity *fluctuated* away from its longer-term upward trend. The compilers of the index took statistics of physical quantities of output, consumption, imports of raw material, transport traffic, etc., and then 'eliminated' the long-term trend. In the following Table the index is shown for years of 'crest' (maximum activity) and 'trough' (minimum activity); to emphasize what this meant in terms of unemployment, the Table also shows un-employment percentages, as annual averages.[2]

As the purpose of this Table is to point the 'cyclical' fluctuations, two episodes have been omitted from the crests and troughs. First, the years 1915-18 were years of high activity (extraordinarily low unemployment) because of the pressure of war production. Second, the year 1926 has been ignored because a dispute in the coal industry, lasting more than half the year, and the connected General Strike in May of that year both directly and indirectly reduced industrial production. One distorting feature, however, has been allowed to remain in the Table: in the post-war period not only was the whole range of unemployment percentages shifted upwards (11 per cent, instead of 2 or 3, in the best year) but the swing from boom (if it could be called a boom) to slump, 1929-32, was more violent than on any pre-war occasion. These are special cases to be recalled in Chapter 4. Meanwhile, a major lesson of Table 5 is that during the sixty years there were eight cycles, with the high points of activity in 1882-3, 1889, 1899, 1906-7, 1913, 1920, 1929, and 1937; the lowest points were generally rather less than half-way between one crest and the next.

Even in the pre-war members of this family of economic fluctuations, the difference between boom and slump was very considerable. The range between high and low in the index of activity was never less than

[1] See Appendix A of *Full Employment in a Free Society* (London, 1944), a classic of the political economy that sprang from contemplation of the trade cycle and the related economic phenomena of 1880-1939.

[2] The unemployment percentages are the well-known trade union series (covering mainly craftsmen) for years to 1922, and the Ministry of Labour index (more comprehensive) for later years.

10 per cent, and in the earliest cycles it was practically 20. This means that in the worst years the nation was producing between four-fifths and nine-tenths of what it might have produced; things were as bad as this at least one year in every decade, and there were other years near the 'trough' when idleness of resources was almost as widespread. What

TABLE 5

Fluctuations in Industrial Activity and Unemployment

	YEAR	CRESTS		TROUGHS	
		Activity	*Unemployment*	*Activity*	*Unemployment*
Trough	1879	..	..	91·0	10·7
Crest	{1882	110·2	2·3	..	..
	{1883	110·6	2·6	..	..
Trough	1886	..	..	89·2	9·5
Crest	1889	107·5	2·0	..	..
Trough	1893	..	..	88·9	7·7
Crest	1899	104·4	2·0	..	..
Trough	{1903	..	..	95·2	5·0
	{1904	..	..	94·7	6·4
Crest	{1906	104·9	3·7	..	..
	{1907	106·1	3·9	..	..
Trough	{1908	..	..	93·5	8·6
	{1909	..	..	94·7	8·7
Crest	1913	108·5	2·1	..	..
Crest	1920	117·9	2·5	..	..
Trough	1922	..	..	88·6	17·4
Crest	1929	118·7	11·0	..	..
Trough	1932	..	..	81·1	22·5
Crest	1937	104·5	11·3	..	..

people consumed, as distinct from what they produced, did not suffer anything like this degree of constriction; total consumption, as far as figures allow a judgement, probably did no worse than suffer occasional checks to its upward trend. The waste of resources, that is to say, had its effect in preventing people from enjoying the fruits of progress, and it checked the expansion of capital equipment at home and investment overseas, thus spreading over a number of years the loss of real income implicit in a single year's idleness of resources. But this mitigation of the material loss resulting from idleness of resources was true only of the nation as a whole, and the unemployment percentages also shown in the

Table call attention to the fact that the idleness meant not only lower production in total but extreme loss of income for the individuals who took the main brunt of depression. Early unemployment percentages represent the experience of a relatively small group of trade-union members, and only guesswork is possible: in the middle 'eighties probably more than one million workers were out of work in the worst months, and in 1908-9 the total may well have been a million and a half, a figure certainly reached in 1922 and nearly doubled in 1932. The fact that total consumption in the nation merely ceased to grow for a year or two was no consolation to hundreds of thousands of families whose sole source of income came to a dead stop. There was meaning in the adjectives when people spoke of the cycle of good and bad years.

The opening of the 'eighties saw the country emerging from a year that had been bad indeed: 1879 had been, through most of its course, the worst year of the 'seventies, and that is saying something. 'One of the most sunless and cheerless of the century' was how *The Economist*'s chronicler characterized it, the description of its weather equally epitomizing commercial and industrial experience. The weather itself, of course, counted for much in those days, and the harvest was 'among the worst on record'. Then trade suddenly brightened, as orders, first for iron and steel and then for many other goods, began to pour in from America, and by March 1880 it was possible to look back on 'a great volume and a great activity of trade'. Thereafter until 1883 the recovery continued: a recovery evident enough in the statistical record, but curiously muted to the contemporary ear. That demand was summoning up almost the full productive powers of the nation is evident in the low unemployment percentages in 1882 and 1883, but contemporary reporters were still using such adjectives as 'dull and dragging'. The farmers were certainly having a lean time, for the weather continued to dog their hopes of better harvests; and agriculture was still so important and widespread an industry that a failure of agricultural income necessarily put the brake on the expansion of markets at home. Part of the farmers' trouble was, however, that overseas sources of food supply had removed the former compensation of high prices for corn when crops were short; while, therefore, farmers might justifiably be groaning at lowness of profits, workers in employment did not now suffer from dearness of food, and could maintain their demand for clothing and other items. In total, demand was much better than maintained, for exports had leapt by about one-fifth and did rather better than this at the peak. With brisk export demand offsetting agricultural gloom, there was some encouragement to industry to add to its equipment, but this boom was not—as were most booms—characterized by any spectacular development of some particular branch of new capital equipment. If a single word is to label it, this was a boom in 'lighting', for the early 'eighties saw a spate of new electricity companies while gasworks were growing apace, and both electricity and gas were as yet mainly for lighting. This was no electricity boom in the sense in which the 'forties had experienced a railway boom; it was just a preliminary flicker, though within our sixty years electricity was to conquer as completely as the railway had conquered in the sixty years before 1880.

By the end of 1884 the country was feeling itself again in depression, but in the early stages it was more a matter of feeling—provoked by falling prices and shrinking profit margins—than of activity. Export trades in general continued to do fairly well, and both the great textile industries held up. The main source of trouble was in shipbuilding and in the metal and engineering trades dependent on shipbuilding. The shipping fleets of the world—Britain's own merchant fleet much the largest among them —were being rebuilt and greatly expanded in this decade, and as a process dependent on long-range decisions of private enterprise this constructional activity was bound to fluctuate severely. In 1881-3 shipping had been one of the main centres of interest in the mania of joint-stock company formations, and the shipbuilding depression of 1884-6 was a normal reaction after that spurt. The metal trades were simultaneously suffering from reaction after another spurt of railway-building in the United States. Unemployment in shipbuilding and the metal industries depressed home markets for other goods, and when in 1885 the cotton industry did less well and the depression made itself more generally felt, the government was driven to appoint a full-dress inquiry into 'the Depression of Trade and Industry'. Perhaps all this talk of depression made things for the moment worse: certainly 1886 was one of the worst years of unemployment, affecting a wide range of industries.

The Royal Commission produced neither a convincing diagnosis of depression nor a cure for it, and the falling tendency of world prices helped to keep British industrialists grumbling for another ten years, but the tide was already on the turn when the Commission reported. Most spectacularly, shipbuilding leapt forward once more, and this industry's activity carried much else with it: iron and steel manufacturers and marine engine builders and a host of others whose market lay in the shipyards of the north-east and the Clyde. This industry seemed to dominate the trade cycle in Britain at this period, and it is worth noting both that it was an industry whose world market was expanding rapidly with the tonnage of foodstuffs and raw materials to be carried from the developing countries across the oceans, and that it was an industry undergoing a fundamental change in technique as sail and iron gave way to steam and steel. After the spurt of 1882-4, the industry was almost prostrate: shipyards stood empty while docks were crowded with idle vessels. Late in 1887 growing demand for cargo space lifted freight rates a little, and the slight revival of demand for new ships was enough to reveal how short of materials the shipbuilders had let themselves become. Then the summer of 1888 was chilly and wet, and it became apparent that much heavier corn imports would be necessary; the shipping world was ready to jump at such encouragement, the shipbuilders' order-books filled, and on the year the industry's output was half as big again as in 1887.

The leap in shipbuilding and in its immediate suppliers soon gave an impetus to the country's trade generally, and at the beginning of 1889 *The Economist* was able to report 'an important improvement in the general trade of the country'. The poor harvest that had given a stimulus to the shipping world was compensated, for the agricultural population, by better experience with animal husbandry. The part played by home agriculture in the trade cycle was becoming both less in intensity and different in its nature; but it was still there, and the bountiful harvest of 1889 certainly helped the liveliness that characterized the country's trade through this year. In addition to sales of new ships—a third of the product of British shipyards was for foreign owners—the export trade was in other things growing fast. Partly because a great flow of British capital was in these years speeding the development of new lands in Australia and South America, world trade generally was brisk, and European prosperity helped to dull the edge of competition. So exports in 1890 reached a level one-quarter higher than at the bottom of the previous depression. *The Economist* held as unquestionable the rapid growth of wealth in the country, and rampant speculation in commodities—cotton, pig-iron, and copper—was paralleled by excesses in foreign investment. But by this time the boom was already cracking: industrialists were complaining of narrower profit margins, Australian prosperity was stumbling, and in November-December 1890 the Bank of England had to come to the rescue of the great house of Baring which had committed itself too deeply in South American finance.

Although with the advantage of hindsight it is possible to regard 'the Baring Crisis' as no merely financial incident but rather as the symptom of temporary over-investment in the southern hemisphere, contemporaries were slow to see that the recent pace of development of new lands could not be sustained and that British trade was bound to suffer from the long pause that ensued. During 1891 and 1892 this position was gradually realized: most of all, the stoppage of railway construction, first in South America and then more widely, hit the export trade in iron and steel goods. The cotton industry suffered from a bad season in India, and new import duties (the McKinley tariff) checked the woollen industry's sales to the U.S.A. The full force of the international depression in iron and steel was felt in 1892, when Australian difficulties were recognized as of the same kind as the South American; these difficulties were destined to become more acute in 1893 and to put the brake on Australian development for many years to come. However, the opening up of new lands in the 'eighties was now bearing its fruit, apparent in the imports of cheap food and materials. This cheap and abundant food had two effects: the volume of the import trade helped to sustain the demand for new ships, and the home market for clothing and other goods benefited from the reduction in expenditure on food. Subsequently the continued depression of export markets—especially in metals, engineering, coal, and cotton—led employers to cut wages, and these cuts, as well as the associated strikes, brought into home trade the depression that had begun as a slump in exports. Two bad years for agriculture—in 1892 a harsh spring and wet harvest, then drought in 1893—intensified the depression. By 1893 even the shipbuilders were using only two-thirds of their capacity, and engineering enterprise at home and abroad seemed 'almost entirely arrested'.

The bottom of the depression was reached in 1893, but 1894, when the new countries remained in financial difficulties and farmers at home had to cope with floods, was almost as bad, and it was not until the middle of 1895 that revival became perceptible. The year 1895 had opened grimly enough: a war between Japan and China depressing Far Eastern markets, another poor season in India, and at home one of those Arctic winters that occur three or four times in a century. (An ox was roasted on the frozen Thames at Westminster.) Then, in the second and third quarters of the year, export business revived: after a revision of the U.S.

tariff American buyers made up for lost time in the woollen trade, and the Far Eastern settlement helped the cotton trade. Engineering and metal industries revived, partly under the impetus of better trade in the outside world, while development of electric lighting and the fashion of the bicycle called for engineering capacity of new kinds.

The new phase of expanding activity lasted until 1899-1900, and was an unusual one in its swing back and forth between home trade and exports. While exports had been important in getting revival going, it was expanding home trade that maintained it, in the face of exceptionally adverse conditions in export markets through 1896 and 1897. British agriculture had good crops in 1896, and quite fair crops in 1897 when prices were forced up by crop failures in other countries. Among these crop failures, India's was most devastating: in two successive years famine was widespread, followed by only one fair season (1898) before famine stalked the land yet again. To compensate such drags on Britain's export trade, shipbuilding and its attendant engineering trades did better, with renewal of the pressure to use more efficient ships, and more naval building as international rivalries began to warm up. Most of all, perhaps (we must be guarded, for in this field we lack comprehensive figures), these years saw a great increase in house-building. Low interest rates and cheap food are great stimulants to the demand for housing (as proved again forty years later), but in those days the capacity of the building industry, typically a craft industry organized by little men, responded only slowly, and it was not until 1896-1900 that the stimulants present since 1892-3 had their full effect. Investment at home was unusually important in other directions, too: electric tramways and the first London 'tube' railway. Of all the booms in the half-century before 1914, this was the only one that was obviously a boom in the development of Britain rather than of other countries.

When export markets improved in 1898 (in India and elsewhere a return to normal after bad crop years), on top of this expanding business for the home market, 'boom' was the only appropriate word; of 1899, *The Economist* could write: 'Seldom has this country enjoyed a year of such all-round activity and prosperity.' The Boer War had broken out in September 1899, and government demands for war material were superimposed on the full pressure of home and export trades; the iron and steel industry enjoyed 'phenomenal activity' and coal went to famine prices. It was unfortunate that these extraordinary pressures forced prices so high just at this time, for early in 1900 the American boom collapsed and British producers were exposed to severe price-cutting from the American iron and steel industry, now far bigger than the British. Then the Boxer troubles broke the Chinese market, and famine the Indian market, for cotton goods. However, these adverse elements in the situation were largely temporary and, though powerful enough to prick the boom, they did not plunge the country into depression either so deep or so prolonged as those of the 'eighties and 'nineties. At its peak the boom had carried prices and profits unusually high and, when the change came, businessmen were able to adapt themselves by narrowing their profit margins. By 1901 India was recovering from the famine, and the Boxer troubles in China were over, so Lancashire was having an altogether better time. Over the country as a whole, it was fairer to say that the tide was on the ebb than that there had been any disastrous slump. The building trade, slow to develop its output in the middle 'nineties, was now just as slow to turn downward. The pressure eased in shipbuilding, but there was no real depression until freights dropped sharply in 1902, partly because war in South Africa effectively ended in May 1902. For once, the domestic elements in the genesis of a boom had been strong enough to maintain much of the impetus long after the export tide had turned.

Between Queen Victoria's death (January 1901) and the outbreak of the European war in 1914—the period to which a generation of Englishmen looked back as a golden age—the tale is one of continuation of the Victorian succession of trade cycles, but in some important respects these years in the new century had an economic climate altogether different from that of the last decade of the old century. The 'nineties had seen a long interruption in the flow of investment in the developing lands beyond the oceans, but Englishmen were enjoying the fruit of earlier efforts. The flood of cheap food and raw materials from the new lands kept the cost of living low, and when a boom did come it was sustained, in unusually high degree, by investment in building at home. The new century saw a sharp contrast. Renewed overseas development of one kind and another (some of it had a militarist flavour) was fed by an unprecedented flow of capital from Britain; but a price had to be paid, in scarcities of commodities, for thus speeding development at a time when the world's productivity had been slackened by the earlier pause in overseas investment. In one direction after another there appeared bouts of pressure of demand on available supplies. Scarcities now of this commodity, now of that, forced prices upward. The cost of living rose, and interest rates rose too, a combination doubly removing the basis of the building boom in Britain itself. This was no phenomenon of a short trade cycle: the volume of building went down and down, the total amount being at least halved during the ten years following its peak in 1902-3. Meanwhile, Britain's huge lending to the outside world was made possible by expansion of the industries that had become traditional exporters: coal, iron and steel, engineering, and textiles. Even more than in the late Victorian decades, employment in pre-1914 Britain was dependent on the world's appetite for these industrial products.

These broad conditions characterized the entire 1900-14 period. Against this background, activity had its vicissitudes from year to year, much as in the 'eighties and 'nineties. The stagnant conditions of 1902, 1903, and 1904 can be regarded as a cyclical phenomenon in that they were largely a reaction to the booming conditions of the previous years; but the booms in different industries had not synchronized at all completely, and the succeeding depressions therefore overlapped rather than coincided with each other, producing a mixed over-all picture of patchy conditions, getting neither spectacularly better nor spectacularly worse: a period, in short, of doldrums. The international depression in iron and steel had begun as early as mid-1900, and recovery was appearing (first in the U.S.A.) from mid-1901. Cotton exports were helped by the settlement of China from 1901 onwards. Export trade generally was helped by the splendid harvests enjoyed in many countries, though Australia was crippled by drought. Shipbuilding had held up longer than other 'war' industries, and its worst year was not until 1903. The building industry at home, with its much longer, slower cycle, was still going up, and turned down slowly in 1904 and 1905, when other industries were enjoying better times. What impetus there was in the more favourable of the 1902 conditions was quickly lost in a combination of adverse circumstances in 1903: a very wet season gave agriculture a disastrous year, a relative shortage of raw cotton impeded production in the Lancashire industry, and the Chamberlain agitation on fiscal policy perhaps, by its pessimistic picture of Britain's competitive position, discouraged investment in industrial equipment. Income-tax went to its peak of 1s. 3d. in 1902-3, and there were increases in taxation of sugar in 1901, of tobacco in 1902 and again in 1904, and of tea in 1904: total revenue was up from £140 M. in 1900-1 to a maximum of £161 M. in 1902-3, and commentators (*The Economist* among them) were probably right in thinking that these increases were reducing the amounts spent on the products of home industry. (A later generation would have argued against such financial policy in time of slack trade, but in 1900-5 the balanced budget was an overriding aim.) Through much of 1904 conditions remained the same, with home trade poor and much pessimistic talk. Late in the year there was some improvement: the cotton market in the United States eased, helping Lancashire, and India and Australia were recovering from the trials their climates had set them in the first years of the century. Then the United States' iron and steel demand picked up, and by the end of the year signs of expansion were becoming less uncommon. The following year (1905) saw widespread and rapid recovery.

The boom that reached its peak in the first half of 1907 was essentially an international boom, in which Britain participated largely because world demand for her great export industries was expanding rapidly from late 1904 onwards. In 1905 more settled international politics and splendid harvests gave foreign trade its impetus. As the volume of trade expanded shipping freights went up and shipbuilding both for home and foreign owners played a leading part in the extreme phase of the boom. The high prosperity of the U.S.A. and Germany in 1906 was especially important in helping the iron and steel and other industries in which those countries were important sources of world demand. The demand for coal was drawn upward as these great devourers of coal—shipping, iron, and steel—prospered. In the later stages the textile industries were feeling the benefit of a brisk home demand on top of good export demand. In all these ways the boom was thoroughly traditional; but the mark of a new century was visible in the boom in rubber for tyres and in nonferrous metals for electrical goods.

By the autumn of 1907 there were many signs of a downturn—commodity prices especially were showing it—and then an American financial crisis and poor harvests in many countries precipitated the onset of depression that lasted through 1908 and most of 1909. The immediate causes of bad trade in 1908 were the sharp slump in the U.S.A., the crisis of Japanese trade consequent on the contraction of silk sales to the U.S.A., and the failure of the Indian harvests. Thus once again the origins of the trouble were in Britain's overseas markets, and the trades most severely affected were those selling to the U.S.A., shipbuilding which reflected the general contraction of world trade, and most of all the cotton industry whose Indian and Far Eastern markets contracted sharply. The more general depression of home trade followed from the fall in incomes earned in these export trades, and was aggravated by the strikes resulting from wage-cuts in them; agricultural purchasing power was maintained by a satisfactory harvest at prices that had been kept up by crop shortages in other countries. The revival can be dated from about mid-1909, following recovery of the U.S.A. from the worst effects of the financial collapse: the first signs of improvement in Britain followed from the revival of export orders from America. Orders for Lancashire goods automatically revived as India recovered from her bad year, but the industry was hindered by shortage of raw cotton following a short crop in the U.S.A. Thus the U.S.A. influenced British trade through conditions of supply of its raw materials as well as by its fluctuations in demand, though over the British economy as a whole it was the transatlantic waves in demand that mattered most. The general revival that followed in Britain failed to stem the depression in the building industry, which continued its decline throughout the tremendous tide of prosperity that was for the next four years to flow through the great export industries.

The boom of 1910-13 was the more remarkable because, although clearly an export boom, it appeared to gather impetus through 1910 despite the slack conditions in the U.S.A., Germany, and some other European countries, and despite growing political tensions both domestic and international. Production was also handicapped by severe industrial disputes, with an increasingly militant labour movement protesting against the pressures of the rising cost of living. The favourable factors were two: the concentration mainly on Britain of the demand for more ships to carry the rising volume of world trade, and the exceptionally rapid development (helped by the flood of British overseas lending) of India, Canada, Australia, South Africa, and South America. The shipyards already in 1911 passed their record output of 1906; in the *three* years 1911-13, the total of new construction was larger than it had been in the *four* good years 1899-1902. This was mercantile shipping, virtually all now built of steel. In addition, Britain and other countries were racing each other in naval construction; this, like demands for the armies of the world, was adding to the opportunities for the steelmakers of the north. British farmers did relatively well, though 1910 was shockingly wet and 1911 a year of drought; but it was the prosperity of farmers in the distant continents that did most to support the demand for Britain's products. In 1912 many of the adverse circumstances, in despite of which Britain had been prospering, disappeared: the U.S.A. and Continental Europe went ahead once more, and abundant harvests elsewhere much more than compensated for a drowned harvest at home. Shipping freights leapt up even faster than before (27 per cent rise on the year); iron and steel, coal (despite a strike), and cotton all enjoyed fantastic prosperity. The Birmingham area, helped by 'a regular boom' in motor-cars for both home and export, enjoyed a foretaste of the engineering booms of fifty years on. Even the building industry felt the backwash of the general prosperity, though it remained a relatively depressed industry.

The boom continued, with production breaking all records, through the first half of 1913, and many statistical series show the year as a whole as the peak, although activity had noticeably slackened long before the year's end. The turn came first in the iron trades, at mid-year; shipping freights collapsed in the autumn and 'new tonnage commenced' turned down sharply enough to bring the year's total below those of 1911 and 1912. These changes resulted from deterioration in the international economic situation: in Canada and the U.S.A. there was some reaction after the feverish trading of the previous year, and European energies (in France, Germany, Austria, and Russia) were being rapidly diverted from production to the training of armies. A partial monsoon failure in India, followed by a banking crisis there, helped to put an end to the cotton industry's boom, though not until the closing months of the year. Even so, the intensity of the previous boom had been such that domestic trade continued to benefit from a high pressure of spending. At Christmas, in the Birmingham area, for instance, notwithstanding the local impact of the downturn in the iron trades, money was reported to be circulating 'fast and furiously'. Coal-miners had a record year, farmers did tolerably well, and the nation was finding that, after years of economic growth, there was something of a backlog of building to be done.

These and other factors, preventing any dramatic collapse of activity, continued to operate through the opening months of 1914: foreign trade was declining and the pressure of spending at home had clearly ceased to mount, but the unemployment percentage at midsummer was still only 2·4. After a boom of such magnitude, the gradualness of this depression was unusual: it contrasted with the downspin of 1907-8, and was a mere ripple by comparison with the collapses that were to be experienced in the post-war world. How this particular trade cycle was working out is, however, one of the hypothetical questions of economic history, for at the end of July the international political pot that had been so long a-simmering suddenly boiled over and Europe was plunged into four years of war. Luxury trades collapsed, exports of cotton and other goods were knocked by the general disruption of the world's shipping, but in the autumn the factories were flooded with British and Allied orders for clothing—and especially boots—and the shipyards were ringing as naval and mercantile repairs were added to the pressure for new tonnage.

The violent break in political history at 1914 is not fully matched in economic history. The likenesses between pre-1914 and post-1914 will be apparent in the next chapter; particularly we shall see how the British economy remained exposed to the fever of the trade cycle. There was, however, some change in the economic climate, a change more radical and more abrupt than that which distinguishes the period 1900-14 from the late decades of the previous century (see p. 38 above). It is therefore fitting that we should at this point break the chronological survey and stand back for a moment to reflect on the characteristics of the waves of alternate prosperity and depression as Britain had known them between 1880 and 1914.

The clearest impression of all is that the British cycle of good and bad trade practically always turned on what was happening in the outside world. Mostly—but not in every instance—the first indication of a turn in the tide was a turn upwards or downwards in the flow of orders for exports to the U.S.A. It is perhaps surprising that a market taking 13 per cent of British exports in the 'eighties and only 7 per cent in the 1900s, should have had this importance; but it was again and again this market that brought the turn of the tide. The British cycle followed the American cycle, though this was a little less true in 1880-1914 than it was either in the period before 1880 or in the inter-war period. The trade most obviously affected in this way was the iron and steel group; this was an international trade, with American and German producers sharply competing with the British, and the experience of one quickly became the experience of all, whether the phase was of good, bad, or indifferent trade. International prosperity—and especially a bout of enthusiasm for constructional development anywhere in the world—infected this trade and, because it was a large British industry, increased the spending that could be directed to the miscellany of goods and services on which people exist. International prosperity had enormous impact too—and this was one of the most spectacular phenomena of this period—on the shipbuilding industry. Ships took a long time to build, and much longer to wear out, so that comparatively small changes in the cargoes to be carried about the world had quite disproportionate effects on freight rates and on the attractions of adding new ships. Britain was easily the world's leading shipbuilder, and took the full force of these fluctuations in demand. Moreover, the techniques were changing fast: changing to the steel steamship, and from the crude early steam engines to the much more efficient engines that were constantly coming from the designers' drawing-boards; this circumstance made shipowners quick to jump out of each depression, for new ships were much more economical to run than the older vessels that had been rusting in the estuaries through a spell of slack trade.

The textile industries also were highly sensitive to conditions outside Britain. This was true of the whole group—cotton, woollen, linen, and jute—but most of all of the Lancashire cotton industry, importing all of its raw material and exporting (in 1913) at least two-thirds of its output in volume, and much more than two-thirds in value. Lancashire could be —and occasionally was—upset by temporary disturbance of supplies of its raw material, but the disturbances on the demand side were large and continual. Most of all at this period, it could be upset by disasters in India, and disaster could strike the Indian market without any regard for what had been happening elsewhere. India was important for other trades as well; her railways, for example, were great customers of the British iron and steel industry. In the better years of the 'eighties India was taking 15 per cent of British exports, and in 1911-13 the percentage was still over 10; even a partial failure of the monsoon could, by its impoverishment and dislocation of Indian markets, give British industry a nasty shock. It was no accident that the Indian monsoon became prominent in school geographies.

This relevance of Indian weather to British prosperity was a special case of a much more general relevance of the world's weather. Crop yields, reflecting variations in weather from year to year, always have had importance in affecting the flow of purchasing power from the agricultural to the non-agricultural parts of the community. This remained true throughout these decades, but, as we have already seen, in rather a different way. Now what seemed to matter (partly because of its effects on the demand for new ships and for steel for building them) was the level of crop yields about the world at large—in India, in North America, in Continental Europe that was still a great customer for many British products, and increasingly in those 'new' countries which British capital had been fertilizing during these decades. The farmers' year at home was still important; again a little differently, for, with so many of their prices now determined by world markets, high yields unequivocally meant high incomes for all engaged in agriculture at home.

One important industry was odd man out: the building industry. It was a big one, too, employing 700,000 people in the 'eighties, and probably a million in the early 1900s. It did seem to have a cycle of good and bad trade, but it was a very long cycle, neither coinciding with nor having any obvious connexion with the shorter cycle that ruled other activities of the industrial nations. Though its oddities occasioned more frequent remark in later years—especially during the great building depression of 1904-11—the industry's fortunes attracted little attention from contemporary economic commentators. In this it was like many other trades that entered little, directly, into the country's foreign trade, and for the same reason: most good economic statistics were a by-product of the interest of governments, especially of their tax-collectors, and these were most concerned with foreign trade. Builders produced for the home market, and their materials were mostly home-produced; therefore the facts of their experience were missing from the statistical records.

These quirks of economic statistics, and the consequential unevenness of economic commentaries, have to be remembered when an attempt is made to assess and interpret the ups and downs of economic activity through these decades. Possibly if we could see more accurately what was happening in every corner of activity, instead of turning so readily to the statistical records of foreign trade, we should find that building was not the only industry with strong tides of its own, that the cross-currents in the economy were far more intricate, and that no concept of *the* trade cycle could be fitted to the confused picture of the whole. Nevertheless, more than a quarter of the occupied population were employed in the coal, iron and steel, shipbuilding, textile, and agricultural industries which featured so largely in contemporary discussions of the problems of alternating prosperity and depression, and it was not irrational for economists to allow themselves to be impressed by the fortunes of these industries and to find in them a pattern they could label 'the trade cycle'. The phenomenon, looked at from a purely British angle, was dominated by the export position: in a sense, Britain was 'importing the trade cycle' from other countries, particularly from the U.S.A. Looked at internationally—as the international cycle that Britain was 'importing'—the cycle seemed to be more marked in industries making *producer* goods than in those making goods for direct consumption, and both among producer goods and among consumer goods the cycle seemed more pronounced the more *durable* were the goods being produced. Putting these facts together with a study of prices, interest rates, and other financial phenomena, whose swings upward and downward over the years seemed to synchronize with the predominant cycles of industrial activity, the economists evolved more elaborate theories of the trade cycle.

For some explanation of the trade cycle public opinion had now become eager. Complacent though it seems to have been with the strides of material progress, pre-1914 Britain refused to regard poverty as part of a divine order. Led by the minority of a Royal Commission on the Poor Laws (1905–9), reformers now approached the problem of poverty by classifying its causes and attacking these causes, among them unemployment. Unemployment in turn was classified by causes (notably in Beveridge's classic *Unemployment*, 1908), and one important cause was obviously the cyclical depression of trade. Perhaps opinion was so eager to grasp at the notion of the trade cycle that the economists too easily overlooked the shortcomings of their data; perhaps they imputed a greater regularity of upward and downward swing than could have been justified by fuller comprehension of that miscellany of business activity which, like building and services, had few ready-made statistical tables. Before, however, theories could be put to the test of further experience, the country was involved in four years of war and a long period of post-war readjustment. After that, as we shall see in the next chapter, the trade cycle unmistakably reappeared: experience in the 1920s and 1930s confirmed the impressions formed in pre-war studies, and helped to create the political economy from which the Full Employment policies of post-war Britain were evolved.

4

The Battered Economy, 1914–1939

THE WAR OF 1914–18, known for a generation as the Great War, to the confusion of historians who had similarly labelled 1793–1815, was later rechristened World War I. From a military point of view, this was a misnomer, for the territorial involvement was essentially European, but in its disturbance of economic life the war was certainly world-wide. Just how deep this disturbance was to be was not apparent for a long time; the first economic impact of the war, though spectacular, was superficial. This was the financial crisis that developed in the last days of July 1914, a crisis that London experienced as the financial centre of the world. The delicacy of the structure of international payments was all too plainly exposed. Because London's position had for half a century been so strong that men had not been confronted with difficulties of this kind, the situation was ineptly handled and there was for a few days a complete breakdown. After the unprecedented four days' Bank Holiday, however, the pieces were put together again and 'Business as usual' became the slogan. There was also in the first weeks something of a scramble at the food shops, which helped to start off the rise of prices, and some cutting of luxury expenditure (including the employment of personal servants) which aggravated the minor unemployment problem of the early months. Much more serious was the disturbance of shipping and the rupture of trade with the enemy countries of Central Europe. The consequent loss of markets created unemployment, especially in the textile industries, while on the import side the stoppage of beet-sugar supplies from the Continent created the first of the real food scarcities, and more generally the new wartime costs of importing food and materials gave the price level a sharp upward twist.

Nevertheless, once the nation had got back its breath in August 1914, there was no sign that business life was going to be radically changed under the stress of gradual mobilization for total war. For this passive attitude there were two reasons. Though thoughtful people recognized that there would have to be a great turnover of effort from the purposes of peace to those of war, they had faith in the mechanism of the market, believing that the incentives of free enterprise would quickly ensure adequate redistribution of resources in response to the bid of government expenditure. Secondly, almost universally people expected the war to be a matter of months, not years. In this atmosphere, 'business as usual' seemed to be both the way to ensure that war production went ahead efficiently and the sensible alternative to panic steps that would have to be reversed in a matter of months. Government interference with economic life was therefore limited at first to such steps as the prohibition of trade with the enemy, requisition of the railways, and precautionary transactions in sugar and wheat.

Further measures of control and direct government intervention in markets came reluctantly during the remainder of 1914 and most of the next two years. But the pressures that forced action in this piecemeal fashion were cumulative, and late in 1916, when people had ceased to think of the end of the war as near, 'business as usual' gave way to an all-out effort. The pressures bringing about this change of front were three: the munitions crisis, the leakage into the army of men needed for essential production, and the increasing difficulty of maintaining imports. The first of these was really a much more general difficulty of securing a quick build-up of equipment for the Armed Forces, but shortages of munitions provided the spectacular example to muster public opinion in support of new policies under the guidance of new ministerial leadership. (This was the issue on which Lloyd George rose to the top.) Haphazard recruitment for the army in the early days, intensified as the urge to enlarge the army developed, led both to direct interference in the labour market (with scant success) and to measures to cope with shortages arising when the men were not there to make the goods. Shipping difficulties were important in creating shortages of particular materials, especially as initial stocks were run down; besides direct effects on production, these failures of the import trade were one of the major causes of the spiral of prices. These pressures were all being exerted in markets where demand was fed by the inflation of government expenditure, inadequately countered by taxation, and there was virtually no resistance in the shape of monetary control. The consequent rise in the cost of living and the haphazard jumps in some wages and some profits created discontent and industrial strife, conditions in which the government was forced to take further controlling action but was unable to count on that public docility which alone could make mild measures wholly effective.

In these conditions the British economy substantially ceased in 1917 and 1918 to be one in which the employment of resources was guided by the play of market forces. Productive capacity was controlled directly by government departments or indirectly through negotiation with traders and manufacturers. Raw materials, especially those imported, were purchased by the government and doled out to manufacturers for approved production. Prices were more and more widely fixed, the channels of distribution more and more closely controlled, and eventually (not until 1918) rationing of the individual consumer was applied to a lengthening list of foods. Employment was controlled, by Military Service Acts beginning in 1916, by gradual development of a system of reserved occupations, by agreements with trade unions, by direct prohibitions on 'poaching' of labour, and (without success) by prohibition of strike action. The British people accepted all this reluctantly; they were brought to it by the shock of army casualties on a horrible scale, by the totally unexpected prolongation of the war, and by the spectacle of economic injustices, large and small, arising in the profiteering economy of 1914-16.

By the time the end came, abruptly in the autumn of 1918, the economy could be described as totally mobilized for the waging of war. By keeping an abnormally high proportion of the population—especially the women—in employment, by working longer hours, by running down equipment and stocks in many industries, and by curtailing their consumption in many directions, the British people had largely provided the sinews of war. They suffered grievous loss of manpower, but the labour force actually in employment in the autumn of 1918 was much bigger than ever before. The loss of shipping tonnage, and the lowered efficiency of what remained, looked like restraining the nation's productivity, but physical destruction within the country had been relatively slight. From the point of view of peacetime requirements, however, much of the productive capacity was ill-suited, and there had to be a big turnover of resources—'swords into ploughshares'—if the waste of idleness on a huge scale was to be avoided. In the event, there was a remarkably quick reshuffling of the labour force. By April 1919 over 2,400,000 had been released from the Armed Forces, civilian employment of men had risen by 1,350,000 while that of women had fallen by 600,000; in the next twelve months another million left the Forces and civilian employment rose by a further 1,650,000. Within the omnibus category 'civilian employment' itself the turnover from one activity to another had been large. Nevertheless, *dislocation* was proving, and for many years remained, much the most burdensome economic legacy of the war.

Not surprisingly, the initial impact of the cessation of hostilities (Armistice Day was 11 November 1918) was a slackening of activity, for wartime demands stopped abruptly while a variety of circumstances prevented even the most pressing peacetime demands from becoming immediately effective. The political collapse of Central and Eastern Europe restrained orders from Britain's nearer customers, and shipping difficulties stood in the way especially of the more distant; export orders for the cotton industry actually declined. Many home demands, like some export demands, looked pressing enough but did not show in immediate production because there were bottlenecks due to shortages of skilled labour or worn-out plant. Industry could not absorb labour as fast as it was being released, and although hundreds of thousands of women and old people dropped out of the labour force, unemployment was around the million mark in March–April 1919.

Then the great re-stocking boom began: a boom in 'working capital'. Both home and export trade soared, export demand for the less dislocated of the European countries leading the way as trading contacts were re-established and merchants sought to refill the pipelines. In 1919 India had an extraordinarily favourable monsoon, stimulating Lancashire trade especially. Before the boom was over, home demand—also essentially for rebuilding stocks in shops and warehouses—had overtaken export demand, and both had given a stimulus to the replacement of war-worn machinery. When the boom cracked in the summer of 1920, it was failure of export demands that led the way, and the essence of the earlier part of the slump was the exhaustion of the process of rebuilding the world's working capital. In both upward and downward swings the activity of the investment-goods industries lagged behind. In shipbuilding the year 1919 saw plenty of stimulus—the activity of world trade, longer supply routes, port congestion, heavy repair activity keeping vessels off the market—but the peak of tonnage-commenced was not reached until the first quarter of 1920. The ships took nine months to a year in building, so that the tonnage under construction went on increasing right into 1921, although freight-rates had by then been quartered. In iron and steel, production continued to rise until the autumn of 1920. House-building hardly even started. The underlying need for houses was acute enough, after the wartime gap in building while families increased in number, but skilled labour was desperately short and the government had no policy to offset the restrictive effects of rent control. So in 1920 only 15,000 houses were built; in 1921, despite reduction in government assistance, completions reached about 80,000, rising activity in this line serving (by accident) to moderate the general fall in economic activity.

The short-lived boom of 1919-20 had extremely unfortunate effects on the structure of the economy, effects that were destined to colour the economic history of the entire inter-war period. The demand (both domestically and for export) for re-stocking with the accustomed staple products had encouraged the reabsorption of labour in industries that had been greatly expanded in the prosperous years before 1914 and had, in some cases, been further expanded to meet war requirements. Once stocks had been rebuilt, worn plant replaced, and efficiency increased by the easement of bottlenecks, the extraordinary pressure of demand vanished almost overnight, and 'cancellation of orders' became a byword in trade reports. The effects of continuing European dislocation re-asserted themselves, and a new competitive position in world trade—in textiles for the East, particularly—uncovered itself, to Britain's discomfort. The country, with so much of its industrial resources concentrated in unwanted places—in coal-mines, iron and steelworks, shipyards, cotton-mills—entered on a long phase of under-employment, lasting until the world slump came after 1929 to make things a great deal worse. Even where there had been no great expansion of capacity, there had often been exchanges of ownership at inflated prices during the boom, and the resulting financial embarrassments of the new owners, notably of cotton-mills and farms, aggravated difficulties in the long depression.

The initial slump was, by any standards, very severe. By March 1921 the trade-union unemployment percentage reached 10 per cent; then industry was dislocated by strikes, especially a long stoppage in coal-mining, and the unemployment percentage rose to 23 in June. Through 1922 and into 1923 depression continued, and when recovery at last began, it did not push the unemployment percentage below 7 (May 1924). For the next five years Britain remained in 'the doldrums' (Pigou's label), with a hard core of about a million unemployed. This hard core was nearly all in three groups of industries: the war-expanded industries, textiles (hit by the collapse of export trade), and dock and harbour services (also hit by the shrinkage of overseas trade). For a long time people persuaded themselves that these trouble spots would disappear when world trade recovered, and this hope encouraged the government to adopt, as a contribution towards reconstruction of a tolerable framework for world trade, an ill-judged policy of restoring the pre-war gold standard in 1925. An immediate effect of making the pound sterling dearer in terms of foreign currencies was to handicap the coal export trade, already struggling in a glutted international market; the consequent fall in coal prices led to a dispute in the coal-mines which lasted more than half of 1926, brought in its train a ten-days' General Strike, and reduced many industries to an extraordinarily low ebb in the latter half of the year. The later effects of the gold standard policy have perhaps been overrated, but it certainly ensured that when European reconstruction at last went ahead (in 1926-9) and emerged as a resurgence of competitors rather than of customers, British industry should be fully exposed. In 1927 there was a backlog of orders in the heavy industries, after the long hold-up of 1926, and unemployment briefly went below 10 per cent. After this backlog had been worked off, depression renewed its grip on the old industries. These being concentrated geographically— in Lancashire, South Wales, the north-east coast, and the Scottish Lowlands—the term 'depressed area' became established in political discussion. A wage-gap was opening out too: by the late 'twenties, wage-rates in engineering, coal, cotton, and agriculture were much lower than those in building, printing, and on the railways.

In the outside world, activity was increasing rapidly in 1927, 1928, and much of 1929, but with so much of the country's resources concentrated in these comparatively unwanted industries, and with their competitive position aggravated by monetary policy, the British economy was scarcely aware that a world boom was in progress. The low incomes of the depressed areas meant unpropitious markets for domestic industries. New industries, new products were appearing: the motor industry was putting itself on the map (in some odd places such as Oxford and Luton) and there was a minor Stock Exchange boom in 1928 in films, greyhound racing tracks, artificial silk, and plate glass; but the low incomes of the depressed areas, and the monetary conditions arising from the gold standard policy and the Wall Street boom, all conspired to limit markets both at home and abroad, and the splash on the Stock Exchange was not matched by any great employment of real resources in the new lines. There were no obvious openings to which surplus labour from the depressed areas could move, and the world boom came and went leaving that hard core of a million unemployed untouched.

The economic blizzard of 1929–32 was something that struck Britain from outside. It had two major origins: a gradual development of relative over-production of primary commodities, disrupting world trading relationships, and the collapse of a speculative fever in the United States. The latter came suddenly, in the autumn of 1929; the fever itself had, in its monetary repercussions, been a nuisance to Britain, and there were at first some who thought of the Wall Street collapse as a relief. But it precipitated the depressing effect of the deeper malaise of the world's producers of primary products, which had already exerted some restraining effect on American markets; moreover, the American financial system proved too weak to take the strain and, far from providing support for the outside world, closed down on nearly all lending at home as well as abroad. The impact on Britain was at once evident in the level of exports. In terms of quantity, between 1929 and 1931 coal exports fell by a third, iron and steel by more than half, cotton and woollen goods by half; even car exports were knocked down from 42,000 to 25,000.

The prevailing political economy allowed the world's central bankers to try to help by lowering interest rates quickly once the Wall Street bubble had burst, but this did little good when every other circumstance was persuading the world's capitalists to cut lending to countries whose prices and incomes had been geared to a continuing inflow of capital. In another direction political economy could not offer even feeble help: the orthodoxies of the world's finance ministries were all against using government expenditure to stem the fall in demand for goods and services; and in 1929 and again in 1931 the British electorate supported this orthodox view. Thus in Britain, as elsewhere, the fall in export incomes was allowed to have its full effect in reducing demand in the home market. The increase in unemployment was therefore not confined to the export industries. Before the end of 1930, 2½ million people were registered as unemployed; a year later, there were nearly 3 millions of them.

The worst was to come in 1932. The cessation of international lending and the deflationary policies of national governments, each one trying to save itself, had proved too great a strain for some of the European banking systems, and in the collapse that followed, Britain was in September 1931 forced to leave the gold standard and thus to lead the world into a phase of instability of foreign exchange rates to add to the foreign exchange restrictions already appearing. World trade, encountering these new obstacles, declined yet further, and for almost every branch except the cotton trade (where there were special circumstances in 1931-2), 1932 saw even smaller quantities of exports than 1931. In values, British exports had fallen from £729 M. in 1929 to £391 M. in 1931, and went to £365 M. in 1932. At mid-year (1932) *The Economist* could write only of hopes doomed to disappointment, the absence of any sign of 'flattening' in the downward swing of wholesale prices, and the 'common prudence' of the scaling down of dividends.

The clearest full cycle in the inter-war period was from the 'crest'—more truly, the low plateau—of 1929 to the half-hearted peak of 1937. The revival started in 1932, from an extraordinarily low level of activity, with a fifth of the country's employable population out of work. It is not easy to date the revival at all precisely: as on other occasions when depression was exceptionally severe, there were fits and starts before recovery really got under way. The earliest sign was in the textile industries, which staged a minor recovery as early as the winter of 1931-2; but this was an oddity due to a difference between Japanese and British foreign exchange action, which had put Japanese competition with Lancashire at a severe disadvantage through the last months of 1931. When the Japanese yen followed sterling downward at the end of 1931, the advantage enjoyed by British exporters evaporated.[1] That the textile revival did prove something of a false dawn seemed, as the year went on, all too characteristic of 1932. It was a gloomy year for nearly everyone: in large areas of the north and west, where the old staple industries were concentrated, 40, 50, or even 60 per cent were without employment for months on end, and London streets were invaded both by processions of unemployed marchers and by individuals begging for any odd job. As the summer went on and the unemployment percentage continued to rise—against the usual seasonal movement—it was surprising that more people did not turn to desperate remedies. In fact there was no action more desperate than a minor turn towards protectionism in foreign trade, and a hardening of hearts against any premature return to the gold standard: the story was, *The Economist* observed, 'a chronicle of difficulties partially surmounted by improvisations rather than successfully solved'.

Nevertheless, the bottom had been reached: by February 1933 *The*

[1] The episode helped to create the industrial and political resistance to a *rise* in sterling in the early spring of 1932, and so prompted an important innovation in British monetary arrangements (the Exchange Equalization Account).

Economist was brave enough to talk of 'barely arrested decline', and by the second half of 1933 the swing downward in the unemployment figures was pronounced enough to hearten most of the nation. Looking back, it is possible to perceive continuous recovery from about September 1932, gathering pace until 1934, then slower recovery through 1934 and much of 1935, and a final brisk improvement until some time in 1937. Why continuous recovery did begin in 1932-3 is less easy to see. The best that can be done is to point to some movements that were strongly characteristic of the entire recovery phase; these may in their beginnings have given the initial impetus that dragged Britain out of its most severe depression in modern times.

The outstanding features of this recovery in the 'thirties were, in terms of activities, the development of the new industries and the building of houses. In results, the appearance was of increasing prosperity in the midlands and south-east of the country, where housing estates sprawled far beyond the previous boundaries of towns of every size, while the old industrial north-western half of the country continued to languish. Consumption of food and clothing was at least maintained while durable and semi-durable consumption goods, both new and old in kind, found larger home markets than ever before. These features continued throughout the period of recovery; in the later phase, 1935-7, the pace of recovery was supported by its spread in the iron and steel industry and the addition of aircraft manufacture to the list of rapidly expanding new industries. These later changes were partly but not entirely due to the rearmament policy then becoming effective, an impetus that continued, and was indeed strengthened, after the general ebb of activity in 1937-8.

In considering the forces on which this recovery of economic activity was based, it is tempting to give primacy to those most obviously relevant to the housing boom, for much of the other expansion of consumer demand—for electricity, for furniture, for cutlery and pots and pans—could be regarded as consequential on the new houses. An undoubted support of the housing boom was the unusual ease of borrowing (especially through building societies) and the low rate of interest which the authorities had stumbled upon and then adopted as one of the few planks in their policy for recovery. Low interest rates, the economists can assure us, stimulate house-building more than they stimulate most other kinds of spending, and there is no doubt that these monetary conditions did greatly support, and perhaps in part initiate, the housing boom of the 'thirties. Housing had other peculiar supports too: the babies who had survived in greater proportion from the first decade of the century were now growing up, and the number of marriages rose some 20 per cent above the level of the 1920s. There were other features of the housing boom, however, that were not so peculiar to housing, and reflection on them prompts a wider search for the fundamental causes of economic revival. One notices, for example, that people were wanting better houses, that they wanted them in different places (the south-east rather than the north-west), and that they wanted them spaced out more widely. What is more, people could apparently pay for these preferences. Nor was there any sign that other forms of consumption were being sacrificed for the sake of the new housing: on the contrary, there was steady expansion in the demand for laundries, dyeing and dry-cleaning, hotel and restaurant services, and in the entertainment and sports industries.

Some of the features just mentioned offer a clue to the solution of the problem: the shift in the details of the demand for housing, and much of the detailed expansion of consumption, were associated with the development of new industries. Electricity supply and the related branches of engineering, the motor industry, new branches of chemicals (including synthetic textiles and paints), and the radio industries were the more spectacular of these developments, but they were by no means the only ones. These industries were applying the new technical knowledge that had originated, sometimes in Britain, sometimes in other countries, in the late nineteenth and early twentieth centuries: all sorts of electrical devices, radio, the internal-combustion engine, and a miscellany of chemical and metallurgical processes. In some of these branches Britain had been a slow starter, but energetic British industrialists had them well in hand during the more prosperous years of the late 'twenties, and the technical knowledge gained from teething troubles had put them in a good position to take advantage of any growth in markets. That growth came in the home market, fundamentally because the English people got their imported food more and more cheaply between 1927 and 1935. The growth was interrupted by the catastrophic slump in the outside world in 1929-31; once that slump was spent, the new industries felt the benefit of the widening margin the Englishman found in the family budget after the food had been bought.

Since the last great spell of cheaper food (in the last quarter of the nineteenth century), there had been two long spells of development of the great agricultural lands of the outside world: pre-1914 and post-1920

there had been rapid peopling of those lands, and heavy capital investment in them. On top of this, there had been intensification of agricultural
research and diffusion of knowledge of the new techniques. All these
factors were, in the later 'twenties, bearing fruit in a great increase in
supplies of foodstuffs and agricultural raw materials. The terms of trade
turned against the agricultural countries, in favour of industrial Britain:
the Englishman got his food more cheaply in terms of the goods he produced for export. The cheapening of food, with the associated problems
of agricultural 'surpluses', was accentuated when the slump came in
1929. The British Index of Retail Prices of Food went down from 160
in 1927 to 157 in 1928, 154 in 1929, 131 in 1931, and 120 in 1933. This
meant that a family that was spending in 1927 £8 on a month's food
could get a similar 'basketful' four years later for £6. 11s., and in 1933
for £6. This was small consolation to the man who had lost his job, but
for the four out of five who were still in work there was a sizeable and
growing margin for new forms of consumption; and this was where the
new demand came from, the demand for more and better houses, the
demand for buses to go to the shops that used motor delivery vans,
the demand for radios, electric light in the bedroom, a motor-coach ride
to the seaside, and rayon stockings to shimmer along the promenade.

Thus the course of the British economy in the 1930s is to be inter-
preted not by itself but as part of a much longer phase dating perhaps
from the completion, around 1925–7, of the main phase in post-war
adjustments. This post-1927 phase is essentially one of a major turn in
the terms of trade in favour of Britain; the turn not being accompanied
by any appreciable lending overseas, British energies found their outlet
increasingly in the development of new industries satisfying new wants
at home. Basically (and in spite of some superficial influences to the contrary) the great slump of 1929–31 was an event coming upon Britain from
the outside world, interrupting but not reversing a trend that was yet
scarcely perceptible. Although it hastened the cheapening of food, the
slump was so abrupt and violent in curtailing the demand for British
exports that it checked the flow of purchasing power that was sustaining
new developments. In 1931 the British people made things worse for
themselves by cutting wages and voting tax increases that bit deeply into
their new margin for luxury consumption. In 1932 world demand ceased
to fall and there were no further wage cuts or tax increases, but food
prices continued to fall and British industry could again feel the benefit
from rising margins over subsistence needs. The car industry had

C

experienced actual decline for two years, but in 1933 it was already passing its former output record; in the next year both this and building were
way ahead of pre-slump levels.

Because the new industries were located mainly in the midlands and
the south-east, and not in the old industrial areas, an increasing population needed an extraordinary number of new houses, and this need was
the more easily satisfied because borrowing was easy and cheap. Viewed
this way, the housing boom was in part a consequence of the industrial
development rather than itself the basic feature of recovery. Increasingly
in the 'thirties it was the internal-combustion engine that gave the
recovery its special flavour: the country bus and the small family car,
making people more mobile over short distances, affected the structure
of the housing demand and fostered radical changes in retail trade.

As the new industries expanded, their own demands on other industries
grew too. Most obviously this was true of building, which was using
much more cement, more bricks, and the new metal window-frames.
The car industry was drawing on the metal industries, particularly for
sheet steel. Consequently, despite the absence of any really massive
development of capital construction, there was from about 1935 a noticeable revival in some of the older industries, particularly iron and steel.
In this development the new protectionist foreign trade policy (dating
from 1932) was important in ensuring that British industry enjoyed the
main benefit of expanding home demand. This must not, of course, be
counted net gain, for the failure of Britain to import more from abroad
did act as a drag on the recovery of the outside world and so on the
demand for British exports; but in the circumstances of the time this
indirect effect may have been negligible, and the protective tariff probably on balance helped the recovery of British industry.

The protectionist measures of the 'thirties, ending the long reign of
the Free Trade policy, indicate the reaction of Englishmen to the blows
under which the economy had been reeling since 1914. In 1880 one
worker in every five had been devoted to production for export, and in the
years before 1914, in a world developing rapidly with the help of British
capital, the proportion had risen to more than one in four. An economy
thus dependent on overseas trade had been plunged into a long major war
and had learned the risks of exposed life-lines. Then, after the brief
effervescence of the post-war boom, much of the world had turned its
back on the established export industries of Britain, even before the
American crash of 1929-33 made the whole world a bad market. In the

'twenties it was reasonable enough to expect Britain's recovery to come through the world's recovery, but when, through its exposure as an export economy, Britain was battered yet again by the events of the outside world, it was not surprising that public opinion and government policy, like the market forces themselves, should turn the British economy in upon itself.

So in the last years before 1939 the British economy had changed both in its orientation and in the way men thought about its problems. Against the one in four before 1914, the proportion of production going to export was now one in eight, and in the partial recovery from its latest battering the impetus was most evident in new industries producing mainly for the home market. This was a very different world from that of 1913, when cotton, coal, steel, and shipbuilding had set the pace; it was natural enough that men felt driven to the view that Britain must work out her own salvation and not leave herself exposed to every wind from across the Atlantic. Strangely enough, Britain was destined after the Second World War, in a very different world economic climate, to be forced into an unprecedented export drive; when this necessity arose, those new home-based industries of the 'thirties were to play a leading part in the response.

5

Technical Progress and the New Industries

THE ECONOMIC HISTORIAN is concerned with material things, with man's varying success or failure in wringing from his environment the flow of goods and services maintaining his standard of living. The historian is therefore under constant temptation, indeed constant obligation, to try to measure, to put in terms of arithmetic the changes over time in the standard of living. The temptation is sharpened by the increasing profusion of figures, and the economists' growing habit of pointing contemporary issues of policy by precise quantification of national productivity and living standards. But the standard of living is a slippery concept: in a changing world there are logically insuperable difficulties of measurement, and these difficulties become serious when as historians we attempt to span decades or centuries. There is little point in measuring man's living standards by translating money incomes in 1880 and 1939 into bushels of wheat: man does not live, even in a material sense, by bread alone. Variety is the spice of life, and the infinite variety of the means of satisfying wants—in clothing, travel, communication, entertainment, and all the rest—shuts the door on arithmetic whose essence is the addition of like to like. Even the convenient analogy between wheat and bread breaks down, under the inventiveness of the milling engineer (successor to the millwright) and the organic chemistry that decrees a different content for our bread.

This example, of change in the baking of bread and in its very nature, points to the main source of disturbance in the quantitative series on which the economic historian would like to rely. In finding new ways of making the traditional goods and in finding ways of making new things that more attractively satisfy his wants, man's inventiveness is, along with the accumulation of resources, the root of economic progress, of the rise in the standard of living which we should so much like to measure. The inventiveness that is relevant is not just a matter of thinking of new ways of doing things, but of finding new ways that are not extravagant in the resources and efforts that have to go into them. Because of this, it is not unrealistic to think of the process of technical improvement as consisting of two steps: an original idea, which is essentially the product of personal curiosity, and the industrial application of it, when the idea has to be translated into industrial processes and the product begins to make an impact on the pattern of consumption. This is a simplification, for the practical application of the idea itself involves inventiveness and adaptability in devising the equipment required for the new process. Nevertheless, there is a distinction between the two phases, and this distinction, between fundamental discoveries and their major industrial application, is important when we are inspecting a period as short as sixty years. Between 1880 and 1939, and especially in the first half of this period, the major changes in the standard of living were derived fairly directly from continuing large-scale application, not only in England but throughout the world, of the basic technological advances of the previous fifty or hundred years. This does not mean, however, that these decades after 1880 were barren of new ideas. There were important new ideas; towards the end of the period these were beginning to be applied on an industrial scale, but their major impact on the living standards of the mass of the people came only after 1939. The technological changes that were making most difference to people before 1914, and even down to 1939, were the railway, steamship, metallurgical, and textile inventions that had much earlier roots but were only now spreading through the world with the accumulation of capital and the diffusion of technical knowledge. While this was going on, human curiosity was not asleep but was exploring further problems whose solution was again to revolutionize, during the twentieth century, the pattern of consumption. The internal-combustion engine led to the automobile and the aeroplane. All sorts of electrical devices revolutionized first lighting and then power, and led on to radio and television. The new organic chemistry led most spectacularly to the artificial textiles and plastics, but also to a host of other developments in soap, perfumes, drugs, photography, refrigeration, and paper-making.

The list of new products and new processes could be lengthened, and greater detail would bring out the close connexions, the cross-fertilization that characterizes technological progress in a tightly-knit industrial society. The motor-car of 1939, for example, depended not only on the internal-combustion engine, but also on the new high-speed multiple machine-tools that depended on ball-bearings, on the new alloy steels, on plastics for fittings and trimmings, and on electrical power at every turn; and enjoyment of the car depended on better road construction. For many of the new processes new kinds of measuring instruments, and greater precision in old types, were absolutely vital; the production of these instruments in turn was dependent not only on more minute understanding of the physical world but also on new products such as fine metals, plastics, and electricity. Equally, closer inspection of the changes reveals the multiple nature of the springs of technical invention. Curiosity may have killed the cat, but it certainly created the motor-car. Another proverb tells us that necessity is the mother of invention. In the sense that necessity means poverty, history has little to say in support, but in the sense that a technical idea comes most fruitfully in response to the intellectual challenge of some practical problem, the proverb is abundantly illustrated by the story of these years. The tremendous development of world population and industrial production during the third quarter of the nineteenth century created relative shortages of many animal products: the shortage of horns and ivory was a challenge that prompted the evolution of plastics. Not that only shortages were created and creative: the use of heavy oils made petroleum a drug on the market, and attempts to find an outlet for a useless by-product guided the engineers whose work blossomed in the automobile. Similarly, when Australia came to the rescue of the world's need for wool, the consequent glut of mutton in a distant land speeded the search for cheap methods of large-scale refrigeration.

In the examples just cited the problems emerged in different countries and the response to the challenge came more or less internationally. This is how technological progress comes about in a world that is closely knit both by the bonds of trade and by the communication of ideas; it is impossible therefore to write in terms only of British history. This does not mean that the distribution of inventiveness between nations is irrelevant to the history of a single nation's economy: Britain's share of ingenuity certainly had and has a bearing on the swing to and fro in the balance of the competitor-customer relationship between Britain and her trading partners, to which attention was directed in Chapter 2. But the international character of technical progress does mean that the story must be told as an international story in which Britain had some part, and this is most emphatically true of the development of the motor-car, the first of the major innovations in these decades.

When we look round for the origins of the motor-car—which, of all the innovations, has done most to give the twentieth century its mechanical character—a trap awaits us in the language of the trade. The words *automobile*, *chauffeur*, and *garage* are all French; but this is accidental in everything but telling us that the French happened to have taken the lead for the brief moment when cars were the fashionable toys of the wealthy. Whether the view is extended backward to the phase when the car appeared as the fantasy of crackpot engineers, or forward to the years of mass production that overturned the world of transport, the story is international. The more fundamental of its two aspects is the invention of the internal-combustion engine; the other is the work of the engineer on the transmission of power to the wheels, the elaboration of steering gear, and all the other elements of mechanical engineering that have gone into the evolution of the modern car.

The internal-combustion engine, like the steam engine, grew from the idea of harnessing the power imparted, in some way, to a piston in a cylinder. Actually the most primitive experiments in internal-combustion engines preceded the steam engine, for attempts to harness in this way the explosive force of gunpowder date back to the late seventeenth century, when the English, French, and Dutch were trying out the idea. They had little success, and the idea was laid aside when the use of steam-power became practicable. In the first third of the nineteenth century, however, when coal-gas was becoming important in England, the basic idea was revived, but using, instead of gunpowder, coal-gas or some similar vapour. These experiments, first in England, were taken up by Frenchmen, and by the 1860s these Frenchmen had laid down the principles of the four-stroke cycle: induction, compression, power, and exhaust. The 'gas engine' was rapidly developed by German engineers; they switched from coal-gas to petroleum residues, and by 1885 Daimler had produced a motor capable of 900 revolutions a minute.

Daimler's motor was used to drive a wooden bicycle; this was characteristic of the genesis of the motor-car, for it was from the cycle trade that many of the mechanical engineers were drawn for the development of the motor-car, and it was in the improvement of the cycle itself that some of the crucial devices were evolved. England, Scotland, and France had all contributed, in the first half of the nineteenth century, to the development of the bicycle, but really rapid progress came only in the 'sixties, when doctors were recommending townsmen to take exercise in cycling and an Englishman returning from France rode one of the latest French machines into the works of the Coventry Sewing Machine Company at a time of slack trade. Coventry leapt to a leading position in cycles, and the production of wire-spoked wheels, chain drives, ball-bearings, and the pneumatic tyre, during the 1870s and 1880s, had immense importance in making possible the motor-car of the twentieth century. It was not only the devices themselves: a vital ingredient in the technical revolution was the raising of a new breed of men, the cycle engineers at Coventry and all over the country. The new figure, with his knack of putting bicycles together and pulling them to pieces again, appears in one of Kipling's stories: 'If you hand him a drum of oil and leave him alone, he can coax a stolen bicycle to do typewriting.' The quotation is not quite apt, for actually the English were relatively slow at making typewriters, and the bicycles handled by a little man in the street at Oxford were not stolen but came in for repair. But the men who liked to tinker with bits of wire, wheels, and cranks, and switched easily from sewing machines to bicycles and from bicycles to motor-cars, were the engineers of the new technological revolution as surely as were the millwrights and clockmakers who made that earlier industrial revolution which provided the title for Professor Ashton's volume in this series.

The position of the cycle business as progenitor of the car gave Coventry an early lead in the new industry, with Daimlers as the first firm of any size. But, though the manufacture of cycles had been fairly concentrated, cycles could go wrong and need repair in hundreds of English towns, and wherever men were trying to put cycles right, a motor engineer might appear; because of this, the early motor industry was scattered over dozens of towns in a way that seemed oddly haphazard to industrial historians whose studies had concentrated on the highly localized industries on the coalfields. Nor were sewing machines and cycles the only progenitors of the motor industry: in the early 1900s Wolseleys switched from sheep-shearing machines to cars, and Napiers, whose products had ranged from cranes to hydraulic machinery and from printing-presses to telescopes, became one of the most famous names in motor engineering before passing on to aero engines. Before there was room for all these firms, however, other changes had been necessary to encourage the demand for cars: in particular, the law had to be revised and the roads had to be made more traffic-worthy.

The law had been an obstacle, in an Act of 1865, said to have been instigated by railway and horse interests fearful of the development of 'steam carriages' on the roads. Under this Act every road vehicle had to carry a crew of two, to run at not more than four miles an hour, and to be preceded by a man with a red flag. This crippling legislation was perhaps a major reason for development of cars at this stage on the Continent rather than in England, but when Dunlops had produced in England pneumatic tyres (1888) that could be fitted to French cars, the latter became attractive enough to excite interest in England and agitation against the 'red flag law'. In 1895 the first motor exhibition (at Tunbridge Wells) helped to generate further demands for amendment of the law, and in 1896 the red-flag and crew requirements were repealed and the speed limit was raised to 12 m.p.h.; in 1903 further amendment raised the speed limit to 20 m.p.h. The cyclists meanwhile had begun pressure for better roads, by the formation of the Roads Improvement Association in 1886, an Association that soon drew support from the new motorists' organizations. (The Automobile Association was founded in 1897.) Dust-laying competitions were organized, and road problems became the subject of international conferences. In 1909 a Development and Road Improvements Fund Act provided the basis for government action: the establishment of a national Road Board, a petrol tax and motor-licence duty to provide the funds, and research at the National Physical Laboratory, leading to better tarred roads and more scientific use of road-stone.

Under these more favourable conditions, the new industry grew rapidly in the years between 1896 and the outbreak of war in 1914. In 1904 over 17,000 motor vehicles were licensed, 8,000 of them being private cars. By 1914 there were 265,000 vehicles, and 193 British firms in the industry, none of them yet very large. Before that, through Edwardian years the motor-car had been essentially the rich man's toy: the toy not of every rich man, but only of those with a taste for mechanical things and—in early days at least—a streak of rashness. The lady who could be persuaded to be a passenger went heavily veiled against the clouds of dust, and besides the inescapable chaperone she was well advised to take with her a nightdress and toothbrush, lest an all-too-likely breakdown should occur too far from a railway station. By 1914 much of this had changed: the cars were less explosive, though the ladies' veils were still part of the uniform. At that date, one country town of 16,000 people boasted four motor-cars, of which two were owned by doctors who were thought unusually lively characters. Then came the

1914 war, after which neither the perils nor the social status of motoring were ever the same again, and the motor industry quickly rose to be one of the nation's principal industries.

While the internal-combustion engine revolutionized transport, the use of electricity was revolutionizing power, lighting, and communications in the British economy. In this field, the fundamental scientific ideas had already been in circulation among the world's inventive minds for a considerable time before 1880, but the technical devices that made it possible to exploit these ideas effectively belong almost entirely to the period 1880–1939. In 1880 there was not a single electric power station, nor a useful electric light bulb. By 1939 the country was covered by a single power grid, most lighting was by electricity, industry was using electrical power on a huge scale, and it was spreading in transport and even in agriculture.

As the motor-car drew on the cycle industry, electrical power drew on the hydraulic engineering of the coal and other mines; and as with the car, no one country could claim to be the home of the crucial inventions. For the production of electric power the development of the turbine was the centrepiece. The French had a long history, going back to the Napoleonic wars and even earlier, in experimenting with water-wheels, and the word 'turbine' is theirs. The Americans were interested at an early date: the waste of energy in the Niagara Falls was challenge enough for any engineer interested in hydraulics. In England the challenge was less spectacular but more insistent, especially as the rapid growth of coal-mining presented problems of mine-drainage and of the lifting and transport of the heavy, bulky product of the mines. So it was on one of the great coalfields, where the Tyne, Wear, and Tees rivers provided a reliable source of water-power, that hydraulic engineering was most fully developed; and, given that this was in the industrial part of England where the steam engine had become a commonplace, it is not surprising that it was in this area that the critical step was taken, of marrying steam to the water-turbine, to produce the steam-turbine. This was designed by Charles Parsons in 1884. He continued to improve it, and founded the firm whose products quickly carried his name all over the world. The largest town in the area, Newcastle, was the first to use a Parsons steam-turbine in its power station, in 1889; Cambridge was the second.

At this time the usual means of street-lighting in British towns was coal-gas; in town homes gas-lighting was common, though the oil-lamp and candle which were universal in the villages were still usual in the poorer homes in towns, and were auxiliaries everywhere. The hold of gas was tightening as the incandescent gas mantle, a German invention of the 1880s, came into use. The adoption of electricity had to wait on the invention of a satisfactory glass light bulb. One of the two necessary steps, a cheap way of evacuating glass bulbs, had been taken by the German Sprengel, back in 1865. The second need was for some filament to bear the current inside the bulb. A Russian inventor had partial success in 1871; the American Edison (some of whose other work was much more successful) made some progress, and then in the early 1880s an Englishman, J. W. Swan, met the need by carbonizing a thread of dissolved cellulose. (This invention, incidentally, was also an important step towards artificial silk; the rayon stocking of the 1920s was thus the half-sister of the electric light that shone on the dancing legs.)

The 1880s also saw great advances in the design and manufacture of the equipment for generating and distributing electricity, and the rise of other great names that have continued to dominate the various branches of the electrical industry. Thus Cromptons set up in Chelmsford in 1878, and played a large part in the planning and equipment of some of the first London power stations. S. de Ferranti in 1882 produced a generator of alternating current, which was eventually to become the norm; the firm he established for this purpose quickly became famous as a manufacturer of other forms of equipment both large and small. Altogether, the 1880s saw British inventors and engineers taking an outstanding part in the development of the electrical industry. The transition to the electrical age nevertheless came much more slowly in England than in other countries on both sides of the Atlantic; coal and steam power were relatively cheap here, and the steam engine had a strong hold on the older industries which were not only the biggest but also were still among the growing industries of Britain. There were, however, other outlets for inventive genius, and in the next generation the most striking advances were in means of communication. The electric telegraph was firmly established, and the first submarine cables were laid, before the end of the 'sixties. In the surge of American development between the end of the Civil War (1865) and 1873, Thomas Edison was building on his knowledge of the telegraph to produce the telephone and the phonograph (forerunner of the gramophone). In England, two great names appeared at the same time in telegraphic research: Oliver Heaviside and H. R. Kempe. In the next generation the strides in physical research in the Cavendish Laboratory at Cambridge, associated particularly with the names of J. J. Thomson and Ernest Rutherford, became of immense importance to the world of electrical engineers of whom Ambrose Fleming was among the most distinguished. Their work, combined with that of the Italian inventor Marconi, made possible the development of wireless telegraphy in the years just before 1914, of broadcasting in the early 1920s, and radar and television just before the Second World War. In 1910 the murderer Crippen, escaping on an Atlantic liner, was overtaken by a radio message; in 1935 almost every English home was equipped to hear King George V broadcast on his Silver Jubilee Day; and in 1939 Britain could be provided with a radar warning system just in time for the first German bombers.

In the chemical industry—more exactly, the group of chemical industries, for products and processes are many—the story of these years is no less important but is more difficult to summarize. The play of the human mind, continuing on problems that had puzzled men through the ages, was becoming more systematic as greater prestige was gained, especially after about 1850, by the scientists; knowledge was advancing on many fronts bearing on chemical manufactures. There were, however, particular directions where circumstances forced the pace: as elsewhere, the relative gluts and shortages provided powerful incentives to guide men's curiosity. The shortages were those arising from the pressure of world demand on animal resources, especially those of wild life: most obviously, the crying need to supplement the supply of bones, horns, ivory tusks, and the like, which had provided so much of man's equipment from the earliest times. The gluts were those of unwanted by-products: as men learned to split the constituents of natural materials (animal, vegetable, and, most of all, mineral), some of the products were unwanted. Indeed, some were positively nasty, and with the closer peopling of the land the problems of disposal of unpleasant by-products had become really serious. The scientist, who could at one blow solve a disposal problem and create a useful new material, was a benefactor increasingly welcome in nineteenth-century Britain.

The problem of disposal of offensive residues had been particularly serious in the alkali industry, which produced materials for the manufacture of soap, glass, and paper, and for the treatment of all textiles, as well as bases for further chemical manufacture. Demands for all such products were rising not only with export markets and with increasing population at home, but also with the rising standard of living of the British people themselves. In the thirty years before 1880 the consumption of soap per head had doubled, for example; these cleaner people were using more glass for windows in their houses, and they were using more paper one way and another. More of these things had meant more effluents from the alkali works, and Parliament had intervened, in 1863 and 1874, to give some protection to the people who lived nearby. This restrictive action encouraged the search for less offensive processes, and the rising quantities of waste products were a challenge to the chemists to find uses for them. The outcome was that in the last quarter of the nineteenth century the alkali industry was transformed by the adoption of the Solvay process, displacing the Leblanc process, and by a new variety in the output. Quite different products, including nitrate of ammonia, chlorine, and (with the help of ore from Canada) nickel, were added to the traditional range of soda materials in the great firm of Brunner Mond which had come to dominate the industry.

The books, magazines, and newspapers that were becoming more common in the homes of Victorian England created another pressure on traditional sources of supply and excited new ideas about production of large quantities. The problem of quantities was tackled by drawing into the paper-making industry a wider range of natural raw materials, and these strange materials gave the industry's chemists many a headache. The great advance came when the chemists succeeded in treating bamboo, which had recently, with the opening-up of trade in the Far East, become comparatively abundant. They tried sulphite of lime on it, and their success in making the bamboo usable in paper-manufacture led on to wide application of sulphite to other more plentiful wood and the beginning of the 'chemical pulp mills' in the 1880s. It was virtually a new industry; it was, incidentally, a foundation-stone for the popular newspapers that were soon entering almost every English home. The whirligig of industrial progress had turned a scarcity almost into a glut; the original scarcity itself had been a stimulant to change, but new availability of Far Eastern products and the new industrial chemists and chemical engineers had been in the story too, before ever the Northcliffes and Beaverbrooks could capture Fleet Street.

The critical step in the paper-making revolution had been the success of the chemists in using alternative and more abundant materials to simulate a product that had been known for centuries. In just the same way in textiles, plastics, and dyestuffs, it was the chemists who, using their new understanding of materials, found ways of making marketable imitations of traditional products. In textiles there were, towards the end of the nineteenth century, three lines of approach. First, the silkworm's secret had always been a challenge, and with the new chemical knowledge (especially 'biochemistry') there seemed hope for some easy way to produce in quantity what the silkworm produced on its microscopic scale. Secondly, there was the idea that the relatively abundant cotton could be treated in some way to give it more of the attractions of silk. Thirdly, there was the idea of producing fibres that would have some useful quality not shared by the natural fibres. A fourth approach, not taken seriously until the inter-war period, was the attempt to simulate the more abundant natural fibres, wool and cotton, so as to achieve independence of the natural sources which might be cut off by war or other catastrophe. This last became important in Germany; the early results were not such as to excite emulation in Britain. British scientists did take some part in probing the silkworm's secret; but only the French tried this on an industrial scale, and they failed in the end. The really profitable lines of development emerged from the attempts to improve cotton and to produce altogether new fibres.

The search for new fibres had its origin, as has already been mentioned, in the problems of electric lighting. The work of J. W. Swan on filaments for electric light bulbs led directly into the development of a nitro-cellulose product, by processes dependent on the chemist's understanding of solvents. At Manchester this work was followed up by C. F. Cross and E. J. Bevan, who were attempting to give to cotton some of the attractions of silk ('mercerised cotton' was the direct outcome of this search). In the early 1900s the Coventry silk firm of Courtaulds took up the work of Cross, Bevan, and others, which was now merged with ideas from Switzerland to evolve a usable fibre which became known as viscose yarn and then, more widely, as rayon. With this, Courtaulds rapidly went ahead; they became the main producers in the U.S.A. as well as in Britain, and in the 1920s were responsible for half the world's output. The other half included the product of an alternative solvent process: the acetate rayon that was developed first in the U.S.A. but was soon taken up in Britain. To the public the product of both processes was known indifferently as artificial silk or rayon, and it won popular favour rapidly after the First World War. Coming when war conditions had just raised the skirt-line clear of the ankle, the new material sparked a revolution in women's dress: the skirt-line climbed knee-high and what had hitherto been concealed in a yardage of cottons and woollens now emerged as two limbs opaquely sheathed in rayon. A new industry was born, an industry in which Britain had a leading place.

The plastics industry is technically a close relative of the artificial silk industry, in that its main processes depend on exploitation of the chemist's understanding of solvents. In the first phase the development of plastics was a clear case of the inventor's response to particular shortages. In the third quarter of the nineteenth century the demand for all those useful hard bits of animals—bones, horns, tusks, and the like—had been outrunning the supply, the exhaustion of wild life in the known continents far outweighing the contemporary penetration of Africa. Demand was expanding not only because population was growing but also because new wants were appearing: in a small way, the dentists were becoming reconstructors instead of mere extractors of teeth; and in a much larger way the whole range of electrical work was going to demand insulating materials here, there, and everywhere. English, Americans, and Germans were all in the hunt; Englishmen and Americans were successful in producing celluloid in the 1860s, and its use became widespread in the remaining decades of the century. Casein was produced accidentally from sour milk, in Germany in the late 1880s, and was soon substituting for ivory, tortoiseshell, and horn. In 1909 the third of this group of new materials was produced from formaldehyde and phenol: it took its name, bakelite, from its American inventor, Backeland. All these plastic materials had great potentialities beyond their original role, and they were soon being widely used, especially in the newer industries, where hardwoods or metals would previously have been essential. By the 1930s the scientists had learned much more of the principles that lay behind these developments and the industrial chemists had come to think of their task as juggling with the molecules to produce an endless series of plastic materials, each one tailored to its particular purpose. The new synthetics were about to change the face of the world's rubber trade, and nylons and drip-dry shirts were just round the corner.

Another line in which the early twentieth century saw nature supplanted by organic chemistry was the production of dyestuffs. In this, Britain notoriously lagged behind: in 1914 the British soldiers went into action in France and Belgium wearing uniforms whose khaki colour depended on imports from Germany. The major advances during the nineteenth century had been made in Germany, where industrial chemists were experimenting with the hydrocarbons that had become so plentiful as by-products of coal-gas. The most important single one of these innovations was probably the synthesis of alizarine, which freed the world from dependence on madder, besides providing the basis for a much greater variety of reds and purples than had previously been possible. The second success of intensive research was the synthesis of indigo from benzene derivatives; in the early years of the twentieth century this synthetic product began to replace the vegetable products of India and Java. Again, as with the alizarine synthesis, the variety of colours was widened. German chemists had come to England in the middle of the nineteenth century, bringing with them some of the early ideas in this industry, but their only practical legacy was the firm of Levinsteins, founded near Manchester in 1864. Here there were some minor developments, including the production of magenta and Blackley blue, but by 1880 the production of this and the four other dyeworks in the country totalled only £450,000, compared with £2,000,000 in Germany. Disruption of this trade by the outbreak of war—a disruption affecting not only home consumption and the clothing of the army but also the export-potential of the great textile industries —shocked public opinion, and the next few years saw a succession of government encouragements for the dyestuffs industry. These steps included subsidies for research, control of imports, and some care for the organization of the industry. As a result, the home industry was by the middle 1920s producing about 80 per cent of the nation's requirements. In the technique of production Britain had broadly caught up with Germany, and new colours were constantly being added to the industry's range; but it was not until the 1930s that technical advance in the British industry could be said to have a momentum of its own instead of just following in German footsteps.

That the British dyestuffs industry did in the end generate its own flow of innovations was most obviously due to the attraction into it, through the governmental encouragements, of chemists whose profession was in twentieth-century Britain rising in public esteem and supported by much enlarged university departments. This background was of course helping other branches of the chemical industry as well. Among those most stimulated were the pharmaceutical branches where the development of synthetic drugs also benefited from their technical relationship with the new dyestuffs, and from the interest of the more scientifically minded leaders of the medical profession. The place of bacteria in diseases was known from about 1860, and known much more extensively from the 'eighties; this knowledge was quickly absorbed by the leading pharmaceutical chemists. There were also attacks on particular problems: especially those of infant feeding. The chemists by 1880 had just found ways of making malt digestible by infants, leading to a great development of production of baby foods, as well as such products as 'malt extract and cod liver oil'. In the twentieth century the foundations of one of the great firms of the industry followed the search for an outlet for dried milk, marketed by a New Zealand firm. The first product had a spectacular record during a gastro-enteritis epidemic in 1911, and the firm was thereby encouraged to press on with its research into the protective agents in milk. The Cambridge biochemist F. G. Hopkins, in the years 1906-12, laid the foundations of our knowledge of vitamins, and the doctors who studied the nutrition problems of the soldiers in 1914-18—and of those whom the army rejected as physically unfit—were particularly important in adding to and in disseminating the new ideas. During the inter-war period, mostly from 1930, British firms were developing one new vitamin product after another, and becoming, along with the Swiss and the Americans, the world's major producers. It was virtually a new industry, still counting its workers in hundreds rather than thousands, but it was the foundation of tremendous development after the Second World War. It was an industry of the new kind, in that its major expense, apart from raw materials, was on its research departments and its commercial and medical advisory services. It was new, too, in its rapid diversification of products: many of its new products never caught on at all, while some of the 'winners' would drop out again quickly as the medical scientists and the industry's own chemists pushed the frontiers of knowledge forward.

Many of the changes in the chemical industries depended upon advances in chemical engineering (the construction of plant for the new processes) to cope with the requirements of exceedingly high temperatures and of precise control of the processes. From this point of view the advances in electrical engineering were often of vital importance: for example, in the development of electric furnaces. No less relevant were the innovations in the metal industries where, although there was no appearance of 'new industries' in the ordinary sense, branches of old industries were revolutionized and became capable of producing the materials needed by the engineers of the new chemical industries. The metal industries have from the earliest times faced two fundamental problems: the production of material that would combine strength with resistance to corrosion, and the problem of joining pieces of metal. In both these directions the first four decades of the twentieth century saw great advances. In the first, there was the development of new alloys, at first only in the steel industry but later in the non-ferrous metals also. In the second, the development of welding made possible much stronger joints consistently with reduced weight.

The use of small quantities of manganese to make steel more workable had been established before 1880 and this general line of attack (of adding traces of other elements to give special properties to steel) was being followed by Sir Robert Hadfield and others through the last decades of the century. Tungsten was being explored as a hardener, opening up new possibilities in machine tools. Since 1872 Frenchmen and Sheffield investigators had been on the trail of chromium as a protective against corrosion, and the breakthrough to the new 'stainless steel' came in 1913 in the work of Brearley, a laboratory worker employed by one of the great steel firms. At first the invention was applied to cutlery, and involved sacrifice of other advantages: stainless steel knives not only did not rust, but also did not cut well, until another ten years' work had been done in the laboratories. By 1921 the new steel was being used for turbine blades for ships, and in 1926 a Firth advertisement described the product as 'the ideal material for chemical boilers and vats—nitric acid plant—brewing machinery—textile machinery—automobile radiator shells, hub-caps and windscreens—food production machinery —sugar-refining plant—tubes for condensers—tanks—domestic hollow-ware'. By 1928 it had become important in machine tools, for which tungsten-carbide alloys had been specially adapted. The high-speed machine tools now possible were of critical importance for mass-production of cars. In the 'thirties the general principles of the alloy tailored to a particular purpose were extended to the non-ferrous metals such as aluminium, lead, and copper. Alloys with traces of the rarer metals—beryllium, tantalum, columbium, etc.—were used as their peculiar properties were recognized. An important newcomer to the field was boron, used in making a very strong steel with high resistance to corrosion and abrasion.

Contemporaneously with the appearance of the new alloy metals, men were finding a new answer to the jointing problem. Some electric-welding processes were known in the U.S.A. by 1900, but the breakthrough in Britain came when automatic electric welding was patented by an engineer in Portsmouth dockyard to meet difficulties originating in the increasing violence of naval warfare. Vibration and shock from gunfire caused rivets to work loose, so creating tiny (but numerous) leaks in riveted bulkheads. The attraction of a jointing method that fused the metal sheets together was only less for merchant ships, and the economy of time and arduous labour encouraged its adoption in shipbuilding generally. Extension to other metal and engineering industries followed, electrical engineers being among the first to take it up. X-ray testing of welded structures helped to generalize its use in the 1930s: thus does one innovation feed upon another. In the late 'thirties a novel application was in the 'hard-facing' of metals. On particular parts of a metal structure a coating or edge of a highly resistant metal could be welded: thus minute quantities of scarce metals could have their peculiar properties exploited while the main structure of a machine consisted of cheaper (and more suitable) metal.

Among these developments of industrial technique, leading to the rise of new industries and the transformation of old, many found stimulus, as we have seen, in the imbalances of supply and demand that arise in a growing economy. There were also, when a major war came in the twentieth century, particular upsets of supply and demand caused both by the war itself and by post-war readjustments, and these imbalances likewise influenced the direction of technical progress. This was most obviously true in the motor industry and its younger brother, the aeroplane industry; with them went the rise of the petroleum industry and a manifold development of new hydrocarbon products. The new solvents industry that grew at Hull and elsewhere in the inter-war period almost began from the necessity of getting rid of surplus war stocks of certain materials. It was thus that five products derived from the fermentation of molasses—ethyl acetate, amyl acetate, butanol, acetone, and acetic acid—became more plentiful and found uses in rayon, varnishes, explosives, leather manufactures, synthetic resins, confectionery, perfumery, cosmetics, measuring instruments, and a host of other products. The war had also influenced technical progress by prodding the British people into greater activity, and more organized activity, in scientific and industrial research. Industrial research associations, government departments, universities, and private firms all joined in the movement. Before 1939 these activities were already bearing fruit in some of the industries referred to in this chapter; but they were also laying the foundations of the great acceleration of Britain's industrial development that was to come after the Second World War.

Meanwhile the innovations already applied in British industry were changing the life of the people not only by providing new products but also by providing them with different work, much of it in industries that were either entirely new or greatly expanded. A few of these changes in employment can be noticed in official statistics, for the unemployment insurance schemes (in post-1920 Britain) had some interesting statistical by-products. Electrical engineering and manufacture (of all kinds) grew from nothing in 1880 to 145,000 workers in 1923 and 341,000 in 1938, as well as a good proportion of the 222,000 engaged in 'gas, water, and electricity supply'. The manufacture of motor vehicles, cycles, and aircraft, virtually non-existent in 1880, employed 192,000 in 1923 and almost 400,000 in 1938. 'Silk, artificial silk, and hosiery' is a group about which we cannot be so categorical; there was a silk industry employing 72,000 people in 1875, and 40,000 in 1907, when there were many thousands making hosiery, but none at all in 'artificial silk'. Employment in the group (now including hosiery) rose from 37,000 in 1923 to nearly 80,000 in 1938, and probably most of these 80,000 were making artificial silk and products thereof. For chemicals we may surmise employment of some 50,000 in 1880; in 1923 104,000 were employed, and in 1938 113,000 with much higher output per worker. In paper and paper-board manufacture (where also output per head was up substantially) there were 56,000 in 1923 and about 67,000 in 1938. In 1880 some—hundreds rather than thousands, one would guess—were employed in making 'scientific and photographic instruments and other apparatus'; in 1923 there were 18,000 of them, and 40,000 in 1938.

These industries just cited were together employing well over a million workers in 1938, and most of this employment had appeared since 1914. Until this date (the beginning of the First World War) the old industries had continued to absorb more and more workers, even though new industries were taking a few of the growing labour force. After 1914—more strictly after 1920—the great industries of the nineteenth century lost workers quickly. Cotton, employing perhaps 500,000 in 1880, had 562,000 employees in 1923 and less than 400,000 in 1938: about the same (in 1938) as motors, cycles, and aircraft. The woollen group had 240,000 in 1923, 216,000 in 1938. Iron and steel, despite a big recovery of output after 1935 and the help of 'the new metallurgy', was in 1938 employing 200,000, against 211,000 in 1923. In 1880 Britain had half a million coal-miners; in 1923 about 1,200,000, and in 1938 858,000. Many other declining industries, being small, have no separate record; but the Ministry of Labour did record 28,000 for 'carriages, carts, etc.' in 1923, and only 13,000 in 1938.

Besides the change of employment by industry, the working lives of millions of men and women were changed by the new kind of work demanded in both old and new industries, though much more in the new than in the old. To the Ruskins of this world technical progress too often means the displacement of individual craftsmanship by the soul-destroying monotony of the factory. History is not as simple as this: it is difficult to believe that in the clothing industry, for example, supersession of the East End seamstress by the Yorkshire factories of the new multiple tailors has increased the destruction of souls. More will be said of the conditions of employment in a later chapter; meanwhile, we may note the bare fact that advancing industrial technique was changing the kind of work men and women had to do, even where industrial classifications were not changing. The milkman ceased to hold the reins and ladle out milk from a metal churn into the housewife's jug: instead, he became the driver of a light motor van, from which he carried the bottles to the housewife's step without ringing the bell. The 'carrier', jogging along for three hours taking the villagers ten miles to market, was succeeded by his son who drove the country bus over twice the distance in half the time. The riveter in the shipyard, a skilled man with heavy work under difficult conditions, was followed by the electric welder. As the most common blind-alley occupation for boys round the London docks, 'van-boy'—the boy who assisted the lorry-driver—was in the 1920s overtaking 'brush-and-pan boy'—the boy who swept the road after the horse-drawn van had gone by. The rag-and-bone man, quite important to supplement raw material supplies in the days when animal materials were becoming scarce, disappeared from the streets when the organic chemists had created the new synthetics. If he had had ambitions for his son, likely as not he would have dreamed of his 'going into an office' as one of the great white-collar brigade. The numbers of these white-collar workers increased enormously during the period; but, with the advances in textiles and clothing and the general rise in incomes, distinctions in dress were becoming blurred and the office stool was losing its attraction. The man of the latest phase was rather the man in the laboratory: it was the white coat, rather than the white collar, that was the insignia of superior employment in the new industrial Britain.

6

Four Export Industries

FROM THE NEW TO THE OLD. While new techniques, new materials, and new wants were drawing a million workers into the new industries of Britain, other industries, already of major importance before 1880, were growing, then stagnating, and—some of them—declining. Of these older industries, four demand particular attention. The iron and steel industry, coal-mining, shipbuilding, and the cotton industry employed between them a million people in 1880, more than 2 millions in 1913, and 1 million in 1938. They were already of immense importance in the export trade in 1880, and they were the backbone of its expansion to 1913. Their downfall after 1920—mainly but not exclusively in their export markets—was a chief element in the comparative stagnation of the British economy in the inter-war period. Their difficulties created the problem of the Depressed Areas and this problem, more than any other single factor, caused Britain to turn its back, in the middle of the twentieth century, on the economic policies inherited from the nineteenth. These four industries cannot, however, be treated as a single group: each of the four has its own particular story, and we therefore devote this chapter to a study of each in turn.

Iron and Steel

The iron and steel industry is an old industry in more senses than one. The working of iron for making implements goes back into the mists of prehistory; its emergence indeed gives the name—the Iron Age—to the last centuries of pre-Roman Britain. More pertinently to the purpose of this book, it is an old industry in the sense that its transformation from medieval ways to a large-scale modern industry was complete before 1880. At this date it was already employing 360,000 people, whose output appeared as 8 million tons of pig-iron before being further processed (within 'the iron and steel industry') to emerge as wrought iron, cast iron, or steel, that would serve as raw material for engineering and other industries in Britain and abroad. As compared with 'the new industries' reviewed in the previous chapter, the iron and steel industry changed relatively little during the six decades 1880-1940; but there was some change, and both the change and its relative slowness had, in such a large industry, important bearing on the living standards the British people could afford. This importance derives partly from the sheer size of the industry, second only to cotton among Britain's manufacturing industries; but also, since Britain's living had come to depend on her position as 'workshop of the world', developments in the iron and steel industry had important implications for the balance of the dual competitor–customer relationship between the British economy and other countries, discussed in Chapter 2.

In the twentieth century the industry has generally been known as 'the iron and steel industry', but latterly the shorter form 'the steel industry' has been becoming usual. Behind the change of wording lies a change in substance, for whereas in 1880 less than a quarter of the iron emerged as steel, in the 1930s the tonnage of steel output actually exceeded the tonnage of pig-iron by 50 per cent, the home-produced pig-iron being supplemented by steel-scrap and imported pig-iron and steel for further processing. From being in 1880 mainly a producer of iron, the industry had by 1939 become primarily a producer of steel. In quantities of the intermediate product pig-iron, figures for the 1880s were much the same as in the 1930s, though they had been a little higher in 1913. British steel production, by contrast, had been multiplied by seven between the 1880s and the late 1930s. This switch to steel as the main product of the industry contributed, incidentally, to the tendency to vertical integration—the agglomeration, in a single plant, of successive processes—and to the consolidation of much of the industry in the hands of large firms which were already dominant early in the period. Technical progress can have far-reaching effects on the structure of an industry, not always conducive to rapid progress in the next phase.

The switch from iron to steel as the main product towards the end of the nineteenth century was essentially due to the response of users to the relative cheapening and improvement of steel that resulted from the technical inventions of the previous generation. Steel and the various kinds of iron are materials consisting of the chemical element iron with small quantities of carbon and other elements; the exact composition (particularly the amount of carbon), and the method of making, produce the variations of strength, hardness, workability, and resistance to corrosion, properties that are of high importance to the engineering and other user industries. For most purposes steel is preferable to iron, though for some goods the comparatively cheap 'cast iron' is adequate, and for others the purer though softer 'wrought iron' is still (in small quantities) used. Steel had been known—produced by accident—from very early times, but before the nineteenth century production was limited, by both raw material and technical conditions, to small quantities. Between 1850 and 1880 three great innovations, associated with the names of Bessemer, Siemens, and Gilchrist-Thomas, had made large-scale production of steel possible and had greatly enlarged the range of ores that could be used. Relatively both to iron and to goods in general, steel cheapened through the last decades of the century, and it was rapidly adopted by those gluttons of iron, the railways and shipbuilders. The technical innovations *after* 1880 were, in the main, responses to the new situation in which most of the pig-iron had to be converted into steel. Once more we find that a group of inventions creates a new supply-and-demand situation and that this change of economic balance provokes a further burst of invention.

Both the main stages in the production of steel—the smelting, which results in pig-iron, and the steel manufacture, which uses the pig-iron as its main material—involve the use of very high temperatures to bring about chemical reactions transforming iron ore into a relatively pure metal whose remaining 'impurities' are precisely controlled. The tonnages used in the world are very large: in the early 1880s world production of pig-iron was around 20 million tons, and by 1939 it was 100 million tons. The materials—iron ore, coke (obtained from coal), and limestone—are available in large quantities all over the world, though the most useful concentrations vary greatly in their chemical contents, and therefore in the problems involved in their utilization for iron and steel manufacture. The processes involve very high temperatures because the separation of the various chemical elements depends on the different melting-points of different elements and compounds: in iron-smelting, for example, the function of the blast furnace is to provide a flow of molten iron that can be drawn off, with relatively little of other material, at the bottom of the furnace. In these high temperatures some of the raw material comes off as gases, and one of the great technical changes in this period was the utilization of these gases, hitherto waste products. In transforming pig-iron into steel, great heat has again to be applied, to a mixture of limestone, iron ore, steel-scrap, and pig-iron, the proportions of these materials being varied according to their several chemical and other properties, their relative availabilities, the particular process being employed, and the particular properties required in the steel that is to emerge at the end of the operation. There are two main variants in the steel-making process, the Bessemer and the open-hearth; both these subdivide according to whether or not use is made of the Gilchrist-Thomas method of eliminating phosphorus by the addition of a basic material, such as limestone, to the pig-iron put into the converter, and the lining of the converter itself with similar material. (Some iron ore has little phosphorus and the Gilchrist-Thomas device is then unnecessary.) Since 1880 a third main method, the electric furnace, has been added, where the heat is created electrically and the contents can be more accurately controlled. The Bessemer, open-hearth, and Gilchrist-Thomas methods had all been devised in the years 1856–78, and much of the earlier history of the industry in this period is the story of adjustment to the application of this new knowledge both in the outside world and in Britain. The electric furnace, by contrast, became of critical importance only in the later decades; from the start it was a vital factor in the development of the new ferro-alloys already referred to in Chapter 5.

The Gilchrist-Thomas device was of great importance in shifting the balance in international competition to Britain's disadvantage. The materials used in the industry are of great weight and bulk, some of which is lost in the process. The sources of the materials have therefore great attractive power in the location of the industry, so the steel industries of the world in consequence tend to be located close to workable beds of rich iron ore if coal and limestone are at hand. The existence in Britain of such materials in mutual proximity was one of the reasons for Britain's lead in the industrial revolution, and the localization of firms within nineteenth-century Britain was clearly related to the geological map. But there are two economic implications of this. First, as the natural deposits of iron ore and coal are worked out, the materials become more expensive and the local industry loses its advantage. Secondly, changes in technical knowledge can change the relative attractions of ores from different places, because their chemical compositions are different. Both these implications were important for the British industry during this period. Particularly, the Gilchrist-Thomas device (the 'basic' process, it was called) had made the phosphoric ores of Germany and Belgium much more usable, and this was a principal reason for the German industry's tremendous growth while the British grew only slowly. British makers were slow to exploit the new method, but this was not due to conservatism: such British phosphoric ores as were available had not quite the same content, in other respects, as the Continental ores that proved so suitable, and 'basic' steel was slow to win a good name for itself among British engineers. The American industry was also going ahead much faster than the British, partly because their market, near at hand, was expanding so quickly but also partly because the abundance of their ore supplies was realized. It was not, however, just a matter of the ores and the coal being there; it was also a matter of how they were handled and transported. With such heavy bulky materials technical efficiency in handling and transporting can make a world of difference to the cost when delivered to the steel-works, and there is no doubt that Britain was laggard in this, so accentuating her competitive weakness *vis-à-vis* the North American producers, and to some extent the Continentals. Here again, as with the adoption of the 'basic' process, Britain's laggardness was partly because British conditions—the exceptionally close proximity of certain materials—limited the advantage of the new methods; but Britain may have been too reluctant.

Certainly the British industry was follower rather than leader in the technical developments within the processes of the industry itself after 1880. There were three main developments: (1) the invention of chamber ovens, much more economical of fuel, for producing the coke, and the utilization of the gas generated in the coking process; (2) the cleaning of the gases in the blast furnaces, by water-washing or by electrostatic methods, so making these gases usable; (3) the invention of an internal-combustion engine which could use the cleaned gases (from the blast furnace) to generate electricity for processing ('rolling') steel. These developments, all tending to get more useful products from a given initial input of coal, were mainly the fruit of German and Belgian research. Britain, used to thinking of coal as so cheap, came along behind. As their coal became dearer, the British firms were in the end driven to adopt these new methods; indeed eventually the best British practice fully rivalled the Continental. Before it could do so, however, the steelmasters had to make more use of the scientists. It was an industry slow to recognize the importance of the industrial chemist: whatever had been true earlier, the iron and steel industry in late nineteenth-century Britain was one where 'the practical man' thought of himself as the only useful pebble on the industrial beach, and it was not until well into the new century that the works laboratory achieved a status appropriate to an industry whose processes involve nice adjustments of chemical content and physical transformation. By the early 1900s, however, the British firms were interesting themselves more positively in the new ways of their Continental competitors, and in 1905 and 1906 there were big installations of the new types of coke-oven. The use of heat generated from one process to supply a subsequent process was driving the industry into putting all the processes together and passing the pig-iron directly, in its molten state, into the steel furnace. In 1913, 28 per cent of the pig-iron used for steel-making went molten to the steel furnace, and by 1924 this percentage had risen to 45.

These developments were substantially reducing the amount of coal required to produce a ton of steel, and this implied a lessening of the attractive power of the coalfields. At the same time the partial exhaustion of some of the British ore deposits and their replacement, as sources for the industry, by rich imported ores led the industry towards the coast. The gravitation coastwards was encouraged further by the relative strength of the shipbuilding and export demands in the generation before 1914: the steelmakers were both getting important raw material supplies from across the water, and putting a large proportion of their products on the water. (In 1913, 30 per cent of Britain's steel output went into shipbuilding and marine engineering, quite apart from steel exports.) In South Wales the old works had been high up in the valleys, and the tendency was to replace these by modern 'integrated' works down near the coast. The north-east coast most of all was, down to 1920, gaining on the inland areas.

Around the turn of the century the industry began to 'come into politics', a tendency that was to be carried much further in the succeeding decades. Although the steel sections were doing well in the better years, Britain was startlingly losing ground by comparison with Germany and the U.S.A. Moreover, international trade in iron and steel was still at this period characterized by severe bouts of price-cutting in the bad years; the organization of the German industry facilitated 'dumping' of a disruptive kind. Arguments about this industry therefore featured in the Tariff Reform movement in the opening years of the twentieth century. In 1906, however, the British electorate, scared by the dear food argument (influenced, too, by quite different issues), turned down the Protectionists, and the steel men had to live in a Free Trade system for another thirty years. As it happened, they did very well through the first two of these three decades. In the years 1904-14 output and exports of both pig-iron and steel reached new high levels. The world's population and trade and machines for making more machines were all increasing fast, and the British industry, especially by using increasing amounts of imported semi-finished steel, secured a share which though declining relatively was expanding absolutely. The structure of the British industry changed little; production steadily gravitated coastwards, however, and a number of loose price associations gradually took hold, especially after it became clear that the industry could not look to the politicians for protection from the erratic blasts of foreign competition.

Then came the stimulus of war, with its huge demand for armament and munition metals. This was followed by the world's re-stocking boom of 1919-20 (see Chapter 4 above), when the steelmakers like so many others were deceived into further expansions of capacity. The government during the war instigated the construction of twenty-two new blast furnaces; few of these had been completed by the end of the war and many of them were among the thirty-seven completed in the years 1920-6. These were individually bigger than pre-war blast furnaces, and few old ones were scrapped, so that total pig-iron capacity rose from 11 million tons in 1913 to 12 millions in 1927. The demand for steel, over the same period, rose much more, and capacity for steelmaking was expanded from 8 million tons to 12 millions.

Between 1913 and 1927 the industry's fortunes were uncomfortably erratic. At the peak in 1919-20, capacity was fully stretched, and some 300,000 men were attached to the industry. But demand—not merely in Britain, but in the whole world—collapsed before 1920 was out, and recovery, when it did come, came only haltingly. In the early 'twenties, years of chaos in foreign exchange markets, it was not difficult for British industrialists to make a case for protection against foreign competition, and despite the electorate's second rejection (1923) of any general policy of import duties, the iron and steel industry continued to agitate for special help of this kind. A governmental inquiry (the Sankey Committee, not to be confused with the Sankey Commission on the Coal Industry) resulted in deferment of decision on a 'safeguarding' tariff, pending the results of reconstruction of the industry. There was in the event no tangible result of the Sankey recommendations, only desultory discussion, but its report at least marks the beginning of the notion that the problems of the industry called for a national plan rather than piece-meal operations firm by firm. Meanwhile there were some minor advances in productivity. There were three large reconstructions of steel plant, reducing fuel consumption, and the works were able to sell more gas and electric power. These changes helped to keep the British industry reasonably competitive, and Britain was able to take some share in meet-ing the world's rapidly growing demand for steel tubes, for steel in bridges and buildings, and for plates, strips, bars, and rods. This was not enough to put the industry on its feet again, especially where (as in the Sheffield area) capacity had been tailored to the vanished demand for armaments. In the absence of any national organization or policy, the pressure for adaptation came primarily from the banks (including the Bank of England) as creditors, and their plans, often weakened by opposi-tion from shareholders, were not of a kind to revolutionize the technical strength of the industry.

The industry was thus in no state to meet the cyclonic slump of 1930-2, when every steel producer in the world was in trouble and com-petition knew no bounds. The world slump, coming after years of un-employment in the industries that had been the staples of British export earnings before 1914, undermined opposition to Protectionism, and in 1932 the iron and steel industry was granted the protection of a $33\frac{1}{3}$ per cent duty on imports. By 1933 output was actually going up again, and with the assurance of continued protection firms were encouraged to rebuild and add new plant, though the old habit of patching remained characteristic. The new tariff policy, however, carried with it new politi-cal pressure for reorganization of the industry, and the old National Federation was strengthened to become the British Iron and Steel Federation, which was to have an independent chairman. The aggres-sive policies of a new Continental steel cartel spurred this British Federa-tion into applying for further protection, and in 1935 the import duties were raised to 50 per cent, which enabled the Federation to make a bargain with the European Steel Cartel. Centralized selling was extended in the export trade, and centralized buying of materials (scrap and ore) was introduced in the import trade.

Thanks to the rearmament demand, the rapid growth of the motor industry, and the 50 per cent tariff, the steel industry in the middle 'thirties recovered more substantially in Britain than elsewhere. The supply of steel-scrap—now a more important material—was unusually erratic in the circumstances of this revival, and the political pressure on the industry to dampen the effects of varying costs forced further development of national organization. The political pressure was extended also to the planning of new capacity, in favour of the depressed areas where thousands of unemployed steelworkers had their homes. The extreme case of this pressure—the agitation for new plant at Jarrow —failed, but more subtly this political atmosphere did tend, despite all the pressure for greater efficiency, to hold the industry to its accustomed ways and its traditional areas. To this there was one notable exception: at long last there was resolution to make efficient use of the huge deposits of low-grade ore in Lincolnshire; here a great 'integrated' works of the most up-to-date kind was constructed just in time to add substantially to the industry's power to meet the needs of war in 1939-45. It was a clean break from the traditions that had kept such a grip on the iron and steel industry since the great days when the railway builders of the world had been its customers. And an industry that had once been a strong-hold of individualism and unregulated competition was henceforward a highly organized and protected industry with regulated prices and centralized trading, an industry that had 'come into politics' to stay.

The Coal Industry

Coal-mining is not as ancient an industry as iron and steel, though Shakespeare's Londoners had sometimes warmed their winter evenings with a fire of 'sea-coals', so called because they had come down by sea from Newcastle. On its modern scale, it was a nineteenth-century industry, providing coke for the iron of the Industrial Revolution, and fuelling the steam engines in the factories, on the railways, and in the ships. By 1880, therefore, it had become one of Britain's largest industries —one of the 'staple industries', as people said. Three hundred and eighty thousand men were directly employed, most of them in the coalfield communities of South Wales, the Scottish Lowlands, Northumberland and Durham, South Lancashire, and the 'Yorks, Derby, and Notts'. It was an industry growing at fantastic speed: as recently as the 1850s annual production had been around 70 million tons; in 1880 it was already 153 millions, and in the 'nineties it passed 200 millions, to reach its all-time peak of 287 million tons in 1913. A high proportion went to feed the steam engines of other countries, and all ships touching British shores reckoned to fill their bunkers before leaving. In 1880, 15 per cent of total output left Britain's shores for one or other of these purposes; in 1913, 94 million tons, about one-third of total output, were thus absorbed. Cardiff and the ports of the north-east lived substantially on the coal that went out. These years of climbing production—and especially the years down to 1902—were years of unbounded confidence, with the mine-owners drawing high profits and (as the mineral rights were privately owned) royalties. To own land under which coal was worked was one of the quickest ways of getting rich in the nineteenth century.

The private ownership of mineral rights had probably encouraged energetic development of the industry in its early days, but the piece-meal exploitation of the coal-seams did make for organization of the industry in small firms which could not plan in any comprehensive way the further development of the fields, and—in the hotbed prosperity of the industry—there was little incentive to bring new ideas into the mining or handling of the coal. Right down to 1914 it remained, as Professor Court has said, 'a pick and shovel industry', with underground haulage that was primitive, though freed from the cruelties to women and children that had disgraced the earlier history of some coalfields. The safety measures and ventilation of the mines had been much improved since mid-century, but there was little other change underground. Steel, cement, and concrete were materials that might have been much used for the roofs and props that framed the miner's workplace, but they were hardly thought of before 1900. Most change was at the pithead: by 1900 every good colliery had some kind of mechanical contrivance for screening, sizing, sorting, and washing the coal, though the apparatus was crude as compared with what is used nowadays. In 1903 only the Yorks, Derby, and Notts. field was using electricity on any scale; it spread rapidly thereafter, though not in any revolutionary ways.

The huge output year by year necessarily meant exhaustion of the more easily worked seams. Compensating discoveries of rich new seams were by this time rare events; deep mining of the thick seams under south Yorkshire and Nottinghamshire was beginning, but new sinkings were few, and more coal could in general be won only at the expense of increasing effort per ton. Over the country as a whole, annual output per man employed went down from 403 tons in 1881 to 340 in 1901 and only 309 in 1911; this sharp fall in an important industry contributed significantly to the check at this time to the rise in productivity per head in the British economy. Yet total output of coal soared, to help meet a world demand that went on growing by 4 per cent per annum; the demand was met by a growth in the labour force from the 380,000 of 1880 to 1,128,000 in 1913. Some men came from other occupations and from other parts of the country—in detail their origins had an astonishing range—but a very large part came from the miners' own families, families that were individually large and had survival rates above those of most other workers.

The size of this body of workers and the circumstances in which they lived and worked made the coal-miners a unique community, with extraordinary cohesion. The miners became a serious force in parliamentary politics, one of the strongest sections of the Trade Union world, and in their own industry the embittered contestants of the system of private ownership. The history of the industry—and of much else in twentieth-century Britain—cannot be understood without appreciation of the unique character of this labour force. The siting of the mines was dictated by the physical facts and could have little regard to contact with other parts of the community; in these isolated mining villages the colliery owners had to build and let the cottages. The whole life of the community would be dominated by the mine, and as the boys grew up they automatically followed father down the pit. The exceptionally heavy work ruled out most of the women, and mining villages held no other avenues of employment. The miners' wives and daughters therefore stayed in the home, to an extent hardly paralleled elsewhere in the working classes of this time; to be a woman in a mining community, where the men were all in the same heavy, dirty work, exposed to the same dangers, was a life quite different from any lived elsewhere. Isolated from the outside world, sharing with all their neighbours the irregularities of wages and employment and the anxieties and critical moments of a dangerous occupation, the women added their own intense loyalty to the strong forces binding the men together. In some areas the surroundings of the mines were dismal enough—grimy patches of the England of the Industrial Revolution—but in others there was cleansing contrast between the sweaty darkness of the coal-face and the fresh countryside into which the miner could step almost from the pithead. Most of all this contrast characterized the great South Wales coalfield, where the pits are high up valleys kept ever green by the soft Welsh rain, where sunsets after showers are remembered by Welshmen the world over; a country that through the ages has bred poets and preachers, a country where hymn-singing is a national pastime. Into such an intense and strongly coloured community, immigrants from other counties were rapidly absorbed; it became a community of immensely tight loyalties, ideal ground for trade unionism, and for political fanaticism rather than for compromise with the realities of the economic and political life of a larger nation. As long as the British nation and the outside world held to the extravagant habit of letting half the coal go as smoke up the chimney, this great body of miners flourished in its own way, revealing its character to a wider audience only on the terrible days of major pit disasters. Later, when the bottom fell out of the market, the miners fought, with closed ranks, by every peaceful means they knew, their bitter resistence making 1921 and 1926 two of the worst years in the economic experience of modern Britain, and finally making unthinkable any rehabilitation of the industry in a framework of private ownership.

The turn of the tide became evident at the beginning of the 'twenties, but there had been signs much earlier. By 1900 electricity, which was to be a spearhead not of the supersession of coal but of its more economical use, was already getting a hold in the world, and oil was already being used for a few battleships. The really big change was more economical use, and this was bound to come in a world that was more scientifically minded. It was probably encouraged by the relative rise in the cost of coal: the South African war had run up the demand and the price for coal extraordinarily in 1899-1902, and though there was some easing when peace came, the falling output per man kept coal dear relatively to the prices users had been paying in the 'eighties and 'nineties. In the last years before 1914 the miners, feeling the rising cost of living, sought higher wages; when the employers thought the market could not bear yet further increases in cost, the atmosphere of the disputes, the bitterness of the strikers, and the political overtones were foretastes of what Britain was to experience in the 1920s.

The changing basis of world demand would no doubt have led to gradual deterioration of the industry's position had peace continued for long after the boom of 1913. As things turned out, the change of trend was concealed by the supply difficulties that resulted from the unplanned withdrawal of young men from the mines for service in the Armed Forces. Government control became necessary, and its purpose had to be the maximization of output from a reduced labour force, at any cost. When the men came back from the trenches and the fever of war demand was over, a Royal Commission was appointed and reported in 1919. This, known from its chairman as the Sankey Commission, was perceptive

D

enough to realize that the post-war world was unlikely to allow the industry the easy prosperity it had enjoyed before the war. It recommended that, in order to facilitate reorganization for more efficient production, the mineral rights should pass into national ownership. On the future of the collieries as firms employing the miners, the Commission was divided: the chairman urged nationalization, but failed to carry all his colleagues with him. In the event, the Report was neglected by governments; the industry was allowed to slide back into its pre-war amorphous state, and the miners thought they had been let down by the nation. Against this regrettable backdrop the industry had to face the collapse of the post-war demand, the increasing signs of a long-term drag downwards in the market, and an immediate catastrophic drop in prices. Through the spring months of 1921 the miners struck desperately but in vain against drastic cuts in wages. This could be seen as the inevitable incident of reaction against a boom in which more labour had been drawn into the industry; more truly it was the first hard knock from the world's more economical habits in coal consumption. Between 1913 and 1937 the world's consumption rose by only 0.3 per cent per annum, against the 4 per cent pre-1913, when far fewer mines had been open outside Britain. For other industries, this meant a healthy reduction in real costs, but for the swollen ranks of British miners the change of trend was catastrophic.

There was a slight easing of the downward pressure on profits, wages, and employment in the mines during 1922 and 1923, when first a long strike in the American coalfields and then military disruption of the Ruhr area reduced the competition that British producers had to meet in international markets. Once these temporary factors disappeared, the industry felt the full depressive force of the excess capacity that characterized the coal trade, not merely in Britain but all over the world, throughout the remainder of the inter-war period. Indeed, the British industry felt more than this, for the rise in the foreign exchange value of the pound sterling, under the gold-standard policy, reduced the price in shillings per ton exported, so aggravating the pressure on wages. Since it was still a 'pick-and-shovel' industry, wage-costs formed an exceptionally large proportion (around 70 per cent) of total costs, and any fall in prices led to immediate threats of wage-cuts or increases in the hours to be worked for the former wages. Nor was there any escape by revolutionizing the techniques of mining. The individual firms—there were 1,400 of them—could see only the excess capacity of the industry and the prospect of continuing losses; even if the firms had wanted to mechanize, bitter relations with the men would have made it impossible to secure co-operation in measures that would have been seen as adding to unemployment. So year after year the struggles of a great industry in decline went on: the owners seeking reductions in cost by cutting wages and lengthening hours, and (in order to get these more easily) escape from the system of national bargaining with the men; the miners on their side resisting wage-cuts, clinging to the shorter hours that had taken so long to win, and fighting for the national bargain in which the men of the various coalfields could support each other.

In 1925 renewed fall in export prices forced a showdown. The government bought, with a £20 M. subsidy, a nine-months' respite, during which another Royal Commission (under Sir Herbert Samuel) produced a masterly Report on the industry's sorry plight. Maximum publicity was achieved by sale of the Report at 3d. a copy, an imaginative detail that helped to make this industry the best understood of all the depressed industries. But understanding was not enough in an industry where labour relations hardly existed except in the negative, belligerent, sense. With no radical change in government policy in prospect, the industry plunged into a stoppage that lasted from 1 May 1926 until the closing weeks of the year, when the miners gradually made the best bargains they could on a district basis. The 7-hours' day was lost; from 1926 the miners worked 8-hour shifts, though political action regained half an hour for them in 1930.

Though the miners lost the struggle, the episode had some slight effect in making possible piecemeal measures of reform in the industry in the thirteen remaining years of peace. Public opinion was not ready for any socialization of the industry, but it was now so informed and so shaken that it was prepared to give some legislative aid to schemes produced by the industry itself: coal-mines reorganization Acts of 1926, 1930, and 1938 bear witness. The employers, though insisting on district not national bargains with the men, went the other way when selling coal, and from the end of the 'twenties they were discussing and sometimes actually operating agreements limiting competition between individual collieries and between districts. The effective part of the Act of 1930 greatly facilitated these agreements: the regulation of sales by quotas and the gradual extension of central selling. By these means— carried further in 1938, when international discussions were held with German and Polish competitors—and by the control of output that followed, the further fall of prices during the world slump was checked and actually reversed.

Though they did save the industry from further trouble in wage-cutting, these cartel arrangements did nothing positively to placate the miners: rather, limitations of output were an exacerbation in an industry to which hundreds of thousands of unemployed were attached. Moreover, the restrictive provisions conflicted with the need to increase efficiency. The improved level of prices provided some incentive and some finance for mechanization, and this did at last gather momentum. In 1927, 58·5 million tons were mechanically cut, and in 1939, 142 millions. (Total production 251 million tons in 1927; 231 millions in 1939.) In 1928, 28 millions were mechanically conveyed at the face; in 1939, 134 millions. Average output per man-shift rose by 11 per cent between 1927 and 1939, though virtually none of the increase occurred in Northumberland, Durham, Scotland, or South Wales. By 1938 public opinion was strong enough for a Conservative government to nationalize all existing and future mineral rights; this removed one obstacle to efficient planning of new pits, though the right of an owner to refuse to disclose plans of existing mines remained untouched. Whether the nation was wise to confine so narrowly its intervention in a thoroughly sick industry is highly questionable. In the last year of peace, output amounted to 227 million tons, of which 36 millions were exported. Of the several hundred firms, a large proportion were running on insignificant or negative profits. An average of 600,000 men were employed, their average weekly earnings (taking skilled and unskilled together) being only 56s. For a decade public policy and private pressures had combined to guide young men away from the mines, even right away from the coal-mining sections of the country, and the labour force, of an industry peculiarly reliant on manual strength, was a body of ageing men. Month in, month out, well over 100,000 men who described themselves as miners were unemployed; but scores of thousands of these were now old men, their skill lost and their muscles sagging from years of idleness. Above all, the industry's labour force, employed and unemployed alike, was an embittered body of men, feeling themselves apart from the nation (as indeed they were), feeling that again and again they had been let down by the nation, feeling themselves always at war against employers who should—the miners thought—be displaced wholesale. This was not an industry in which anyone would consider investment of the huge sums that would have to come from outside if methods were ever to take advantage of fifty years of scientific and technical advance. It was a state of affairs for which the nation was to pay dearly during the years of war, and in the ten years of coal-rationing after the war.

Shipbuilding

Though ships have always been built in Britain—at any rate since the Saxons based on the waterways their penetration of the land—Britain's position as the world's shipbuilder belongs only to the last two or three hundred years, and the term is fully justified only for a few decades after 1860. Through the first half of the nineteenth century the yards that lined many estuaries of Britain—including the Thames—were probably responsible for most of the ships that crossed the oceans of the world. Smaller coastal and river craft—not forgetting the Far Eastern junks, which were not so small—were ordinarily built, in many shapes and sizes, beside the rivers that remained their homes; this had always been the way of the world, as in some measure it is to this day. But those who had their business in great waters had increasingly, in the period of the Industrial Revolution, gone down to the sea in ships built around the coasts of Britain. In the 1850s this British supremacy suffered a sharp setback: in Massachusetts and other New England States, where ship-builders enjoyed the advantage of plentiful timber and 'naval stores', the craftsmen went ahead and built some of the fastest big sailing-ships ever built in the world. Through this and the following decades the world enjoyed the spectacle of the races of the 'clippers' bearing grain or tea on the long routes round the southern capes; but this was no more than a last grand flourish of the sailing-ship as an ocean carrier, and with its eclipse the New England shipyards' challenge lost its sting. In their experience of the steam engine the engineers of Britain had a card up their sleeve, and as the wood-and-iron sailing-ship gave way first to the iron steamship and then to the steel steamship the British shipyards again took a clear lead, and retained it for more than half a century. The decisive decade was the 'sixties, when the Americans were spending their energies in civil war and the Suez Canal was built. The Canal was of crucial importance, for it opened to the East a route that could be studded with coaling stations—Gibraltar, Port Said, Aden, and all the rest—a route far shorter than those along which the clippers could drive before prevailing winds. Scattered about the world, sailing-boats like row-boats and other small craft far outnumbered the new steamships, but in terms of tonnage crossing the oceans, it was the day of the steamship, and with it of British leadership in shipbuilding. To this day one can find in far corners of the world odd-looking steamships dating back into the nineteenth century, and they invariably bear the names of Clydeside or Tyneside or other British shipyards.

In 1880, 54,000 people were directly employed in shipbuilding in this country, and a few thousands in marine engineering might well be similarly classed. Neglecting the very small ships, 983 ships were in that year completed, totalling 473,000 tons. Of this total, 822 ships, of 403,800 tons, were built for British owners; the rest were sold abroad. At the beginning of the 1890s new steamships were much bigger than new sailing-ships: 1,600 tons on the average, against about 1,000 tons for sailers, big increases as compared with the average of 500 tons for all kinds in 1880, but still very small as compared with the ordinary 8,000- to 12,000-tons freighter of the middle twentieth century. The proportion of sailing-ships was rapidly declining: by 1900 there were only 28, of 9,871 tons, among the 1,442,000 tons built in Britain, and after that the figures of sailers were scarcely worth recording. The average size of ship rose more rapidly after 1900. Throughout the period this rise in average size was being pulled up by the increase in the size of the giants as well as the average ships: it was an era when faster liners meant ever larger ships. This was true even in the depressed 'thirties, when the meagre total tonnages were helped by the building of the two Cunard 'Queens', which at 80,000 tons seem likely to remain the biggest passenger ships in the history of the British industry.

Between 1880 and the First World War the shipbuilding industry was thus, by exploiting the possibilities of steam-power and steel, making a great contribution both to direct exports (of ships sold abroad) and, by equipping British shipping companies, to their capacity for earning by carrying goods to and from Britain and between other countries. The success was, however, by no means unchequered, for shipbuilding was an industry of violently fluctuating activity. In the 'eighties, for example, the highest annual tonnage built was 1,300,000, nearly three times the figure for the worst year; and between 1900 and 1913 the best was more than twice the worst. This implied, for the workers, a swing back and forth between years of overtime and high earnings and years of short-time and heavy unemployment, and the experience of this industry attracted special attention when the economists began to analyse unemployment and the causes of poverty. The trouble was rooted in a combination of circumstances, the chief being the inelasticity in the demand for shipping services and the fact that ships take a long time to build and even longer to wear out. When, because of booming trade generally or because harvest failures occasion unusually large shipments from distant ports, the demand for shipping space soars, buyers will stand sharp rises in freight rates without turning a hair, and big profits can be earned by companies with ships ready for service. In a world of private enterprise, this excites demand for new ships, but ships take many months, some of them more than a year, to build. Shipping people know the ups and downs of their trade well enough to realize that the good times will not last, but the firm that is first in getting its new ships down the slipway may win a rich reward in a few months. The urge is always therefore to put in new orders quickly when freight rates rise, and inevitably too many ships are ordered. Two years or more pass before all the new ships are in service, and then freights tumble down. Then comes the long end of the economist's 'short period': the glut of ships is not easily relieved by the ships' wearing out. A ship lasts many many years—ten, twenty, or thirty years—before the oceans have so battered her and her engines have revolved so many cycles, that repairs cease to be worth while and the ship is towed away to the breakers' yard. Once a glut of ships has appeared there is, therefore, little demand for new ships until another accident demands extraordinary movement of goods about the world, or the world's normal growth threatens to overtake the capacity of the world's fleets.

There is, however, one important source of relief for the shipbuilders from that depressing long end of the short period. Technical advance—improvement in the art of shipbuilding—can hasten the day when the shipowner feels justified in incurring the capital cost of a new ship. If the shipbuilder can produce a ship that is much more efficient than the older ships ever were, his customers may be persuaded that the drop in running costs would outweigh the capital charges on new ships: that total costs of running new ships would be less than the prime costs of running old ships. The way out of slack trade for the shipbuilder is therefore closely tied up with his ability to increase the running efficiency of the ships he builds; and as international competition increased in shipbuilding—as it did throughout the period—it became more and more important to the British shipbuilder to search out improvements. Improvement might be found in any one of many directions, for a ship is a complex product with diverse properties. The ship has to be strong and swift in carrying weights across the sea; it has to carry its source of motive power, or rely on uncertain winds; it should be stable (cargo shifts alarmingly in ships' holds as well as in passengers' stomachs); a ship must be easily handled in port, and be able to handle cargo and fuel quickly. In all these ways, save one, there were great advances in technique during these decades. The exception was stability: men were tackling this continually, but the line of attack (special tanks inside the ship) proved unfruitful, and it was not until the middle of the twentieth century that success came with the adoption of external 'fins'.

The last decades of the nineteenth century saw spectacular changes in the appearance as well as the efficiency of the ships launched from the shipyards of Britain, for steam and steel were making faster, stronger, and more controllable ships that could carry altogether more cargo than the iron sailing-ships of the previous generation. In 1880 British owners were using 20,000 sailing-ships, totalling 3·9 million tons, and 5,250 steamers totalling 2·7 million tons, but among ships launched during the previous four years the proportions were quite different: 221 sailing-ships totalling 64,000 tons and 932 steamers of 480,000 tons. Long before 1914 the launchings of new sailers had become negligible. The engines for the steamers were rapidly improved: in the early 'eighties the triple expansion engine made its appearance, and then, with exploitation of steel in marine engineering, quadruple and even quintuple expansion engines came in the late 'nineties. These were reciprocating engines, fuelled by coal; improvements continued in them, for in the sixteen years 1911-26 the power extracted from the coal was increased by 15 per cent. By this time, however, the steam turbine had replaced the reciprocating engine for the fastest ships. The first turbine vessel was launched in 1897 and in the 1900s the turbine was rapidly adopted for warships, cross-channel steamers, and passenger liners; in 1910 the geared turbine was introduced.

Steamships—whether with reciprocating engines or turbines—are not necessarily coal-burners. On routes where cheap coal is not accessible, there was opportunity for other fuel. Oil began to replace coal, as the fuel for raising steam, in the early 1900s; by 1914 2·6 per cent, and in the mid-1920s more than a quarter of ships were oil-burning. More radical was the supersession of steam by the internal-combustion engine. This was tried first in an oil-tanker in 1907 and there were a few diesel-engined ships before 1914, but it was not until the 1920s that their much lower tonnage of fuel requirement made the motor ships really attractive. By 1939 a quarter of the world's ocean tonnage was of diesel ships.

Electric propulsion was by then being tried out; some of the few passenger ships built in the 'thirties were 'diesel-electric'. Besides the major task of propulsion, machines cope with many other tasks on board a modern ship; especially the disappearance of former gluts in dock labour has made loading and unloading machinery important, and in this and many other directions turbines and electricity have been used.

As soon as the wind-filled sail had given way to the man-controlled engine, it became really important to assess as exactly as possible the power required to drive a particular ship through the sea. The resistance of the water depends not merely on the size and weight of the ship but also on the detailed shape of every part that has contact with the water. Though paper calculations can help, they do not take the naval architect very far, and the only practical solution has been to run exact models of planned ships in experimental tanks. The Admiralty began serious work along these lines in the 1870s, and a tank built in 1886 was successful enough to secure widespread recognition of the method. Tanks were then built by some of the private firms, and in 1911 a greatly improved tank at the National Physical Laboratory at Teddington became available for use by the private firms. More and more elaborate devices were adopted in studying the movements of these toy-ships in the experimental tanks; particularly, advances in photography helped the designers to understand and to measure the complicated likes and dislikes that waves and water-flows have for the curves and crannies of a ship's bottom. All this more scientific approach to the problems of naval architecture and marine engineering led to many changes, some spectacular and some more subtle, in the shapes of twentieth-century ships; among them the most obvious to the untutored eye is the disappearance amidships of the V-shape, the virtual 'squaring', of the typical cargo-ship.

The efficiency and shape of a ship were also influenced by the material used both in the hull and in the machinery. In the 1880s the change from iron to steel hulls was going ahead rapidly. The steel universally used was mild steel, combining toughness with ductility; it was typically a manganese steel of the kind evolved in that period. In the 1920s, however, the industry began to take advantage of the new 'special quality steel' possessing more elasticity than ordinary mild steel and reducing by about one-tenth the weight of steel required in a vessel of moderate size. New special-purpose steels were rapidly exploited by the marine engineers, notably for turbines. In the 1930s shipbuilders adopted another of the new metallurgical developments: the new methods of welding, enabling them to dispense with much of the arduous labour of riveting, at the same time increasing the strength of a hull of given weight.

With new materials and the more scientific approach encouraged by the introduction of mechanical propulsion, the building of special-purpose ships became much more common. One type of special-purpose ship—the passenger liner—was already well established and was further developed during these decades, but a new chapter began in 1886 when the first 'oil tanker', to carry 5,000 tons of oil, was launched. By 1913 these tankers constituted 11 per cent of the world's output, and then, after the war, the idea was applied to shipment in bulk of coal, ores, and grain. The advantages of these specialized vessels were such that again and again—most usefully perhaps in 1930-1—owners thought fit to order new tonnage of this kind even when the world had far too many ordinary cargo ships.

This incidental effect of the development of special-purpose ships was no more than an extreme case of the effect of advancing technique generally: by offering more efficient ships, the British yards could attract orders even in years when the estuaries of the world were studded with idle ships. By keeping in the lead technically, the British industry could also stand against competition from foreign yards. In this they had considerable success, for in 1913 practically all construction for British owners and a quarter of that for foreign owners was in British yards. This position—much stronger than that of sixty years earlier—was based largely on the advantage British builders enjoyed in easy access to cheap steel, but this, coupled with the increase in the size of ships, had also made for increased geographical concentration of the industry within Britain. The great estuaries that had steelworks at the back door gained complete ascendancy; henceforth, shipbuilding was the business of Clydeside, Tyneside, the Wear, the Mersey, and Belfast. Here were most of the 580 berths from which all ships of any size were launched, and here more than 200,000 people were employed by the industry. This concentration, though essential for the maintenance of Britain's competitive position, had some unfortunate implications, in that, despite the cushioning sometimes provided by technical advances, the industry remained subject to extraordinary fluctuations, the brunt of which fell on people who formed the main population of certain areas. This was bad enough in the expansionary pre-1914 period, when the output of the worst years would be only half that of the best years. But things became much worse after 1921, for the pre-war boom followed by the distortions of wartime had both grossly over-supplied the world with ships and made the capacity of British yards far greater than ever before. The two inter-war decades were therefore characterized by chronic unemployment of shipyards and of men: a large proportion of the men highly skilled, concentrated in a few towns adjacent to areas themselves depressed by the failure of the other pre-war export industries. Even in the best of the inter-war years (1929) nearly half the berths were idle, although Britain was producing more than half of the world's new ships. In the catastrophe that followed, building practically stopped throughout the world. Two-thirds of the shrinking labour force of the British yards were out of work month after month. The Jarrow men marched to London to press for government action: a grim sight, and their march was in vain. Until 1935 the British government (unlike the governments of most of the industry's foreign competitors) would do nothing to help an industry with whose products the world was apparently glutted.

The firms in the industry had, however, been making a concerted attack on the problem of excess capacity. In 1930, the forty-seven firms owning nearly all the yards of any size agreed—with encouragement, perhaps pressure, from the Bank of England—to a scheme for buying and dismantling some of the least employed and least efficient yards, financing their operations by a levy on all new tonnage launched by the member firms. Under this plan about a quarter of the industry's capacity was eliminated during the next few years, while another quarter was forced out by the action of individual companies. These reductions brought the industry's capacity down to a level not much above what had been needed in the better years of the 'twenties, but demand in the 'thirties never touched this. In 1935 the government, goaded by the intensified stimulants administered to foreign shipbuilders, granted special loan facilities to encourage cargo-shipowners to build new tonnage while scrapping twice as much old tonnage. This 'scrap and build' plan prompted a little more building, but the 186,000 tons spread over three years was a mere trifle in relation to the capacity of the ship-yards and the army of unemployed craftsmen still attached to the industry. In the end it was reviving world trade rather than any govern-mental stimulants that pulled the industry up, and in the last three years before the Second World War launchings were not much below a million tons a year. This was comparable with the worst, not the average, years of the 'twenties, and only half the boom levels of 1911-13 and 1918-20; but at least it ensured that there was an active nucleus for the coming years when the demands of the nation at war once again set the shipyards ringing.

Cotton

Of all the 'old industries' which, as industries that lost their expansionary impetus between 1880 and 1940, are the subject of this chapter, the cotton industry is the youngest. In Britain cotton was scarcely known before 1700; the Lancashire cotton industry (traditionally so-called, though it spills over neighbouring counties) was essentially the child of the Industrial Revolution. Through the second half of the eighteenth century, and especially after 1780, it was growing fast; in the nineteenth century it became the main pillar of Britain's exports and one of the largest employers of labour, and its growth put Manchester and Liverpool into the front rank of English cities. The firms in which it was organized were large by the standards of eighteenth-century England, but in the nineteenth they became very numerous and a highly competitive spirit breathed through the industry. This and the extreme dependence on export trade helped to give Lancashire its political flavour, and, as the industry grew, the cotton towns became one of the major forces in English politics, until in the early twentieth century people claimed that 'what Lancashire thinks today England will think tomorrow'. The industry was also notable as the largest group of employed women in the nation: throughout these decades nearly two-thirds of those employed were females, and this meant over 400,000 in the last years before 1914. This was the peak, for total employment in the industry had risen from 520,000 in 1880 to 646,000 in 1911 and then dwindled to 400,000 in 1939 and much less thereafter. Through the 1920s the industry was on the defensive, believing itself the victim of temporary difficulties; even in 1928 the Balfour Committee thought Lancashire retained great advantages. In the 1930s it became all too clear that the trouble was deep-seated, and that cotton's primacy among the manufacturing industries of Britain was a thing of the past. The industry had flourished on the basis of a colossal export trade, and none suffered more abruptly from the competitive aspect of economic development in other countries. In 1929, when world trade was in tolerably good shape, the volume of cotton exports was down to half its

1913 level; two years later it was down to one-quarter and it benefited little when partial recovery came elsewhere.

The industry's business is to transform a vegetable fibre, which comes into the country looking like dirty 'cotton-wool', into cotton cloth which is sold for making into clothes and other household and industrial goods. The main processes in this transformation are (1) cleaning and carding (into distinguishable fibres), (2) spinning (into 'yarn'), (3) doubling (twisting yarns together), (4) weaving (technically referred to as 'manu-facturing'), and (5) bleaching, dyeing or printing, and finishing. In the Lancashire industry in this period the first and second processes were invariably united in the same firm, and frequently the third process as well; firms in this work were referred to as 'spinners'. Some spinners were also engaged in weaving, but three-quarters of the firms did only one or the other. The final processes—dyeing, etc.—were indepen-dently organized, almost without exception. In spinning there was specialization of mills according to the quality of raw cotton used: the 'American' section, much the larger, producing the coarser yarns from American-type cotton, and the 'Egyptian' producing finer yarns from the longer-staple cotton, much of which came from Egypt.

In 1884 there were 1,642 firms in spinning or weaving or both; less than one-fifth of them were joint-stock companies, the rest being family firms and partnerships. There had been a great increase in efficiency, especially in the application of steam-power in weaving, in the 1850s and 1860s, and by 1871 factory production—or rather, in Lancashire's wording, production in 'mills'—was the universal rule. There had, how-ever, been no radical changes of technique, and the central machines— the self-acting mule and the ring frame in spinning, and the power loom for weaving—were basically what had been invented by Crompton, Arkwright, and Cartwright, a century earlier. There was little ring-spinning; it was rather looked down upon, as a producer of inferior goods by inferior labour, and it spread only slowly in the succeeding decades of expanding trade. The technical torpor was more general than this. Mules were modified only in detail, though they, and more parti-cularly looms, became faster and more efficient. An automatic loom was invented by an Englishman but, though extensively adopted in the United States and elsewhere, in Lancashire it was regarded as another of those gadgets suitable for low-grade products that were not the right line for Lancashire's markets. Electricity began to be used for motive power from about 1904, but it crept rather than swept into the mills.

In short, the equipment of mills that were already established by the eighties changed little, far into the new century; this was one of the industries in which the check to the rise in productivity was most marked.

In the expanding state of the trade down to 1913, these old mills, using the familiar mule spindles and power looms, had no difficulty in finding profitable work. Markets in the Far East, which had expanded rapidly just before 1880, remained strong, though subject to serious upsets. African and other new markets were developing, and Europe was taking much more yarn (to the benefit of spinners, though not of weavers) for further processing in its own textile industries. Without radical changes of technique, this expanding demand meant that there was room for new mills alongside the old, and every spasm of brisk trade saw the hatching of a new brood of 'joint-stock' spinning mills: 'the Oldham Limiteds' as they were called in one of the most flourishing districts. The boom of 1905-7 provided the extreme example, when ninety-five new mills, with $8\frac{1}{2}$ million spindles, went up in two years, increasing spinning capacity by nearly one-fifth. These new mills impressed a Lancashire-born historian as 'light and almost beautiful': not that earlier specimens had ever justified Blake's reference to 'dark satanic mills'. They substantially reproduced the conventional techniques, and with 100,000 spindles instead of the earlier 10,000 or 20,000 in a mill, they were noisier than ever, and Lancashire lasses became adept at lip-reading.

Before these new mills were erected, the spinning section had been famous for its dominance by firms of a fairly uniform capacity, 10,000 to 20,000 spindles. This uniformity of size in cotton spinners is said to have lain behind Alfred Marshall's concept of the Representative Firm, but while in these decades the concept was being dinned into successive generations of English students of economics, the reality was already disappearing. For the old mills (now a little enlarged) flourished alongside the new, and by 1911 there were two 'representative' sizes, 20,000-30,000 spindles and 90,000-100,000. The larger type was associated particularly with the joint-stock form of organization, and the 'joint-stocks' were most firmly entrenched in the Oldham district, which produced the more standardized goods for sale in bulk, products that lent themselves most readily to larger units of managerial control. The same tendency could be seen in the weaving section, though it had not gone as far as in spinning. At the high-quality end of the spinning section one mammoth firm appeared: in 1898 The Fine Cotton Spinners and Doublers Association Ltd. had been formed by the combination of thirty-one firms with 3 million spindles, but it was not highly centralized. Altogether, by 1913 the detailed size-distribution of the cotton firms was exceedingly complex; the facts were ever more obstinately refusing to fit into the tidy 'economic boxes' of the theorists.

When the First World War ended in 1918 the traders of the world were all short of 'Lancashire goods' and, as soon as contacts were re-established, there was a scramble to refill the pipe-lines. Lancashire met what first appeared as a bigger and better boom of the old kind, and its reaction, following its own 1905-7 precedent, was to float a number of new joint-stock companies. There was, however, one big difference: thanks to the difficulties of the engineering industries, no quick addition to the industry's equipment was possible. Actually, capacity in the economic sense was reduced, for the industry fully shared in the widespread shortening of hours in British industry. This limitation of capacity probably aggravated the rise in prices and consequently in profits, and the high profits led to the writing-up of capital values by the issue of bonus shares and excited the formation of new companies to buy mills at prices three or four times those previously ruling. The majority of the mills concerned were in the American section, and they included half the spindles in this section; unfortunately, this was the section most badly hit when depression came. The subsequent troubles of these highly capitalized companies were aggravated by the fact that, following the traditional practice of the industry, much of the capital was raised on loan. Companies can declare no dividend on shares in bad years, but interest on loans falls due inexorably, and the embarrassment of these interest payments was destined to be a nagging source of weakness in the industry. It was also unfortunate that much of the money was raised from Lancashire workers who were persuaded by its obvious prosperity to invest their savings in the industry they knew best. Their subsequent loss of capital just when their employment prospects were bleakest provided one of the nation's most grievous examples of the disadvantage of employee-participation in ownership.

The financial reorganization in the boom of 1919 was confined to the spinners, and mainly to the American section of these. Weaving continued largely in the hands of private firms and private companies, and the finishing trades were already largely concentrated in three powerful public companies. Perhaps the company promoters would have got round to the weavers as well as the spinners if the boom had gone on long enough, but in a matter of months the bubble was pricked and Lancashire settled into the gloom from which it has never entirely escaped. The depression was the worse for the coincidence of the collapse of the extraordinary re-stocking demand with sharply adverse trends at home and abroad. At home, fashions were changing fast: women's dresses were shorter and closer-fitting, and much less cloth went into linings and underclothes. The export demand was affected by parallel changes in some other countries, but much more important was the progress of textile industries ever more widely established around the world. When the worst of the world slump was over, these underlying trends remained and were sharpened as artificial silk began to displace cotton and as Japan became a major exporter. Adversity from these conditions was, however, unevenly spread. The attractions of rayon are greater by comparison with coarse cotton goods than with fine; moreover, the Egyptian types of yarn were more usable in combination with artificial fibres, the new demand for rayon stockings involving, for example, Egyptian cotton for the tops. The decline in the export demand also was weighted against the American section, for it was in the coarser goods that foreign competitors first proved their efficiency. So through the middle and later 'twenties the Egyptian section managed on the whole to make a tolerable living. (So did the finishing trades, which could switch to artificial silk and the fine cottons that were doing relatively well.) The brunt of the shrinkage of demand fell on the American spinning section and those weaving firms which were in the coarser end of the trade. Organized short-time, designed to spread the work consistently with benefit from national unemployment pay for the workers, had been the resort of almost the entire industry in the slump of 1920-2, but it became a continuing habit in the American section.

This organized short-time, appropriate enough as a palliative in temporary depression, was seen to be no real remedy as the years went by and markets remained stagnant or worse. Two circumstances had particular influence on ideas of more drastic treatment. First, the cotton men were impressed by the contrast between the comparative affluence of the finishing trades, which were organized in large, almost monopolistic units, and the 'weak selling' and crippling prices accepted in the amorphous, highly competitive spinning section. Secondly, work-spreading measures like organized short-time raised costs, which was exactly the wrong way to meet the permanent sharpening of foreign competition; lower costs should be sought by concentrating production in firms organized on an altogether larger scale. In the relatively prosperous Egyptian section, eighteen firms with 3 million spindles combined in 1929, with some success. The American section, where the need for drastic action was more acute, was a harder nut to crack, but under pressure from the Bank of England (the only obliging banker when others had burned their fingers) the Lancashire Cotton Corporation was founded, also in 1929. This was to include some 200 mills, with 20 million spindles; its intention was to recondition the better of these mills, and scrap the rest, so at once eliminating surplus capacity and raising average efficiency. The process of rationalization proved disappointingly slow: by 1935 only 140 of the mills had been acquired, 74 of which were scrapped, and the Corporation had been compelled to pay uncomfortably high prices for the spindles that were scrapped. While these horizontal combinations were in process, there was also much talk of the need for more vertical integration, especially for trimming the great army of merchants. From 1931 onwards there was a succession of schemes for reductions of capacity; a 'pool' scheme for scrapping spindles was at last agreed in 1936 and an Act of Parliament was obtained in order to override awkward minorities.

Meanwhile, ever since 1922 attempts had been made, with varying success, to limit internal competition by a variety of price-fixing schemes. When the second great shrinkage of demand occurred, in 1930-2, it became increasingly difficult to hold individuals to these agreements, and in 1935 quota systems for sharing output were organized as supports for minimum prices. Still no light showed on the horizon—in 1938 a quarter of the industry's shrunken labour force was out of work—and the industry eventually sought and obtained statutory sanctions for a price-fixing scheme. This was so comprehensive and detailed a measure that a few months later it fitted into wartime price controls as hand into glove. Altogether, in the 'thirties the cotton industry had tried almost every conceivable regulatory device, from simple price-fixing to control of capacity, from loose agreements to complete unification, from private regulation to control by Parliament. Victorian cotton men must have turned in their graves. Certainly all this was a far cry from the doctrines preached in the Free Trade Hall at Manchester, but then, *laisser-faire* never was popular in an industry in retreat.

7
Agriculture

FOR THE INDUSTRIES that were in nineteenth-century Britain the great exporters, the economic development of the outside world remained into the first decades of the twentieth century a powerful stimulant, adding to the pressure of demand for their products. For agriculture the reverse was true; for this, the largest employer of labour in 1880, development in the outside world was a breeder of competition, not of widening markets. Especially the last phase of the nineteenth century witnessed a spectacular development of the world's transport equipment—of ships and railways—and while this brought extraordinary bursts of prosperity and expansion to three of the four industries discussed in the previous chapter, it exposed British agriculture to ruinous competition. The history of British agriculture during all six of these decades, and not only the last two of them, is a story of shrinkage and adjustment under the pressure of a persistent decline in the demand for its products.

In terms of the numbers of people occupied, agriculture had been at its peak in mid-century, when about 2 million people were occupied in farming, forestry, and fishing, the overwhelming proportion being in farming. By 1880 this number was down to 1,700,000, about one in eight of the nation's working population, and the next six decades carried the total down to about a million, one-twentieth of the working population, on the eve of the Second World War. Decline in such a great industry inevitably became a concern of government, the more so from the circumstance that there were intimate ties between agriculture and the landowning classes who in 1880 had still a tight hold on political life. In 1881 a Royal Commission, under the chairmanship of the Duke of Richmond, was busy investigating the depression in agriculture; it was the first industry deemed important enough to warrant (in 1889) a government department of its own, and long before 1939 it had become second nature to the farmers to complain that the government was not doing enough for them. Their complaints were the more vigorous after the 1914–18 war which, underlining the perils of dependence on overseas food supplies, had inspired hopes that were doomed to disappointment and legislation that was quickly repealed.

'Agriculture' is, however, an omnibus word, covering the production of a great variety of products: grains, grasses, and root crops; wool, meat, milk, butter, and eggs; fruit and vegetables. These varied products were not equally or simultaneously involved in the sharpening of competition from abroad, and the demand for many of them benefited from the increasing population which, with rising wealth, was ready to pay for more meat and dairy products, more fruit and vegetables. Farmers in different parts of the country, engaged in different kinds of farming and depending on markets for quite different products, were not by any means equally affected by the flood of imported food. For a time, indeed, some benefited more from the cheapening of food for their livestock than they lost through the competition of imports. This relief did not last for long; before 1900 cold-storage in transport was beginning to hurt the pastoral farmers of the west and north as the grain farmers of eastern England had been hurt a generation earlier. For producers of some dairy products and most fruits and vegetables, the shortcomings of transport gave a natural protection much longer, but it was development of demand rather than absence of competing supplies that afforded the more lasting support. Fortunately for the people on the land, both labour and land can to some extent be switched from one product to another, and as the markets for different products were successively depressed, there was some escape by changes of this kind. But adaptation was often difficult and always left its scars, and when one escape-avenue after another felt the blast of competition the discouragement was cumulative, and by the 1930s the face of the countryside was evidence enough that the industry had lost heart.

From what was being said in London, and in the eastern counties, at the beginning of the 1880s, one would almost suppose that British agriculture had already come to the end of its tether. This was a false impression, current among members of both Houses of Parliament whose sporting habits made them familiar with the cornlands of the eastern half of the country; contemporary opinion was also prejudiced by a succession of bad seasons culminating in the dreadful 1879. Beneath all the exaggerations, however, there was an unmistakably hard core of truth. As railways in the new lands overseas were completed and as shipping costs fell, one agricultural product after another became worth bringing by sea in large quantities. The trouble began with the commodities most easily transportable: wool and wheat. In the twenty years after 1864, imports of Australasian wool doubled then doubled again. The resulting fall in the price of wool affected a great variety of farmers, all over the country, for sheep had a place in the pattern of arable farming in the east and south as well as in the pastoral farming of the west and north; but this was no more than a first dent, and by itself would hardly have forced radical changes. More serious—partly because it came on top of the fall in wool prices—was the fall in wheat. When the U.S.A. settled down after its Civil War (1861-5), that country became a major source of cheap wheat for the English market. Total imports into Britain rose from about 1 million tons in the late 'fifties to 3 to 4 million tons in the early 'eighties, and half of this came from the United States. Imports from the U.S.A. alone, that is to say, nearly equalled home production which was, in the early 'eighties, around 2 million tons in an average season. Australia, Canada, and India between them supplied rather more than 500,000 tons, and in the next decades these sources grew rapidly in importance, while the quantity coming from the U.S.A. changed little except according to good and bad seasons. In the 'eighties and 'nineties the Argentine jumped up to rival India as the second largest source; then after 1900 Canadian and Australian wheat increased most rapidly, so that in the last years before 1914 Britain was drawing from overseas more than 5 million tons, three times the amount then produced at home. The British farmer was managing, that is to say, to hold only a quarter of the home market, and he was able to do this only by accepting prices that for many years had been below 30s. a quarter, as compared with 45s. around 1880. The market for other grains—barley and oats—had been flooded by cheap imports a little ahead of the flood of wheat; the farmer whose chief reliance was on receipts from grain could find no relief by turning from one grain crop to another.

For some years, however, the profitability of animal husbandry was helped rather than hindered by the development of imports. Some live cattle were shipped in from Europe, and there were appreciable imports of bacon and tinned pork, but shipments of mutton were trivial and were only of tinned or boiled meat which could not attract any appreciable proportion of total demand. At the same time, the cheapening of grain-feed for cattle was reducing costs for the pastoral farmers. There was relief therefore for arable farmers who could switch to pastoral farming, and especially in 'mixed' farming where the distribution of land and effort could be changed in favour of the more profitable meat and dairy products. There was unhappily much resistance to the change: corn farmers continued through the poor-weather years between 1883 and 1890 to hope that they could pull round again if only they had a run of average or good seasons, and they and their fathers had been brought up in the belief that the customary balancing of crops and animals was the only farming that on their land could maintain output. Sometimes radical change was made possible by change of tenant, particularly to Scots who brought their economical ideas of dairy farming to East Anglian clays; but the new tenants often had a hard time with their neighbours who, expressing their faith in the old as the only ways that could last, were quick to say 'Scot never follows Scot' when these farms changed hands again. Nevertheless, there was a big transfer: between 1870 and 1880 the acreage under grain crops went down from 9,548,000 to 8,875,000, then to 8,032,000 in 1890 and 7,335,000 in 1900, while permanent pasture increased from 12,073,000 acres in 1870 to 14,427,000 in 1880, 16,018,000 in 1890, and 16,729,000 in 1900.

By 1885 the next phase was foreshadowed by the technical developments in refrigeration of meat cargoes. Hitherto the most distant source of substantial imports had been the Middle West of the U.S.A., but now the Argentine, Australia, and New Zealand could compete, especially with frozen mutton and lamb. By the middle 'nineties, one-third of the country's meat consumption was imported, as compared with one-quarter in the late 'seventies. Total consumption was increasing fast, and the increase in imports was consistent with an actual increase in home production, but the British farmers were able to hold this share only by accepting prices a third or more below the previous level. The overseas competition came just at the time when new pastures, formerly corn land, had come into production, and the effect was to spread over the whole country the agricultural depression that had hitherto been confined to the grain farmers of the east and south. Those who had switched from corn to cattle had switched into a falling market, and by the middle 1890s British agriculture was in a more desperate condition than anyone could remember. Dairying was by this time suffering from the same disease of competing imports: Canadian cheese, Danish butter, and Dutch eggs; and the Dutch had added a manufactured product, margarine. Though prices English farmers received for these products did not tumble as wool, corn, and meat had fallen earlier, only milk remained generally profitable; even this market was eventually invaded by tinned milk from Switzerland.

The upshot was that in the last twenty years of the nineteenth century there was no escape from a sharply downward trend in the farmers' receipts from sale of their produce. A large proportion of the land was rented by the farmers from landlords of the traditional type (half the land in England and Wales was owned by 1,700 peers and other great landowners), and these landlords were obliged to make concessions as the price of securing continuance of any tenants at all. The losses were too big to be absorbed in contraction of the tenants' own incomes and, illustrating Ricardian theories, rents were widely left unpaid or heavily reduced. Over the period, it is believed that rents fell by about one-third. This average figure conceals a wide range reflecting the varying incidence of falling prices, and for some landlords with heavy financial commitments the fall was serious enough to persuade them to sell. The drop in the price of agricultural land at the extreme phase—in the mid-'nineties—was a minor factor in the development of the speculative housing boom in the following years: thus does the working of the market sometimes transform one man's poison into another man's meat. For farming itself the fall in landlords' incomes was damaging, for substantial capital requirements were traditionally met by landlords, and scarcity of capital made changes in farming practice more difficult.

The farmers could get little relief by cutting wage-rates. In the worst years in the 'eighties, there was some wage-cutting in the eastern counties, where town and countryside alike were clouded by the depression; but in the counties that encircled or neighboured more prosperous industrial areas, any wage-cutting would at once have aggravated the drift of labour into the towns. Even in the east, however, wage-cutting did not last long, for every county was hearing the call of the new lands of opportunity across the sea; at the same time, prosperity in alternative employments became more widely diffused inside Britain, and the new trade unionism, though hardly touching agriculture directly, was making wage-rates all over the country more resistant. In short, though they were able to lighten their rent-bills, the farmers were unable to find relief by paying less to each labourer. Even at unchanged wage-rates the drift from the land was averaging 20,000 labourers a year.

Another way to cut costs was by increasing efficiency—by getting, that is to say, a greater quantity of produce from a given acreage and labour-force. Men whose daily work was so close to Nature, so ruled by the wind and the rain, did not readily accept mechanical contrivances, but there were always some experimenters, and as the pressure to reduce costs intensified, the agricultural engineers had more chance. Pirie's plough had arrived in 1863 and was at last becoming popular; it allowed one man with two or three horses to replace two men with four horses. The self-binding reaper, taking on the arduous work of binding the sheaves before stooking, arrived from America and by 1886 its success was generally acknowledged. Minor improvements in threshing tackle allowed faster work and left the grain cleaner. For the grassland, there were new mowers, horse-rakes, swathe-turners, and elevators. For the potato-grower, there was a plough to get the potatoes out of the ground. Little stationary oil engines were appearing here and there, and the travelling teams of threshers used steam-engines; but most of the latest gadgets used horses, and the number on the farms was still just increasing. Advances in the metal industries counted for something in these changes on the farm: better ironwork was improving a wide range of implements, wire became more useful for fences, and the Gilchrist-Thomas process in steelmaking was responsible for a by-product, basic-slag, which, after 1896, became a valuable fertilizer for grassland. The application of scientific knowledge to the problems of agriculture was now a matter of organized effort, at the research station at Rothamsted and elsewhere, and the possibilities of nitrogenous and potassic fertilizers were widely acknowledged from the 1870s onward.

The use of artificial fertilizers was particularly important in allowing farmers to break from the tyranny of the customary rotations. These customary patterns of farming had been a chief impediment to alterations of the balance in favour of the more profitable (or less unprofitable) products, so that the development of fertilizers was peculiarly important in increasing the broad flexibility—and so the profitability in the face of changing demands—of farming. Another kind of resistance was being overcome by governmental interest, and by the discomfiture of landlords. Farm leases often contained clauses designed to preserve the customary pattern; some landlords gave way when they realized how difficult it was to keep good tenants, and a succession of Agricultural Holdings Acts, in 1875, 1883, and 1906, outlawed the more restrictive kinds of lease. So the patterns of farming became, especially in the new century, altogether more flexible. Potatoes, carrots, cabbages, peas, beans, and brussels sprouts—all of them 'cash crops' readily marketed in the nearest towns—were introduced to vary the old-fashioned three- and four-course rotations. Similarly, Parliament, by the Market Gardeners Compensation Act in 1895, reduced the risks of tenants' investment in market gardening. With this encouragement, this kind of farming became the special line of considerable areas in the Thames Valley, north Kent, Bedfordshire, Huntingdonshire, and the Fens. The Vale of Evesham won its name for fruit-growing, as did parts of Cambridgeshire and Essex close to newly established jam factories. Cornwall became a great producer of autumn and winter broccoli, and of early flowers. The tomato ceased to be a phenomenon of the rich man's table and came from glasshouses by the acre behind Worthing, round Swanley (Kent), and up the Lea Valley to the north of London.

This trend towards specialized farming, especially of vegetables, fruit, potatoes, and above all milk, continued after 1900. Though the number of sheep went down, cattle increased just a little and, more productively, the quality of the cattle was improved by the activity of Breed Societies. More meat was being eaten, and home producers saw the profit in high-quality meat, which was still free from overseas competition. The health authorities had become interested in the cleanliness of the cowsheds; it was an age of more and better milk, though still not enough for the children's health. Especially, more milk was going into the towns, with the railways fostering the traffic: morning and afternoon the horse-drawn loads of churns trundled into the village stations, and townspeople began to distinguish between 'farm milk' and 'railway milk'. By 1908 one-fifth of the value of farm output was dairy produce, and milk itself was much the largest part of this, for the creameries of Denmark and elsewhere on the near-Continent had captured the market for butter and cheese. There were a few technical developments in the dairies: milk-coolers and separators were helping, but mechanical milkers were rare until after the First World War, and the dairy-maids worked in much the traditional way. In potato farming—still anyone's business, but also with increasing specialist areas—there was more careful selection of seed, and the introduction of new disease-resisting strains. The area under small fruit crept up to 100,000 acres, and around the towns the fields of vegetables became more common. While agriculture as a whole was continually losing labour, those occupied in market gardening increased: as compared with 1881, the Census of 1911 showed a 25 per cent fall of employment in agriculture, but 'gardeners' and the like increased by 77 per cent. There were also by 1914 a few thousands of 'small-holders' whose landlords were the County Councils which had acted under the Small Holdings and Allotments Act of 1908; most of these men were producing vegetables or fruit.

All these developments were consistent with little change between 1900 and 1914 in the grain acreage. Only barley went down, reflecting the drop in the nation's consumption of beer.[1] In the cultivation of grain crops, the ingenuity of the agricultural engineers was making a steady contribution, enabling the farmers to maintain acreage with a dwindling labour force. In the plough itself, concave mouldboards and the new steels reduced the labour of man and horse. Spring-framed 'cultivators' were making headway all over the country. Mechanical rick-lifters were improved; so were corn-drills, though broadcast sowing was still to be seen in Scotland. The little stationary oil engines were coming in fast, for all sorts of jobs in the barn and about the farmyard; in 1908 there were 13,000 of them, though this meant only one for every twenty farmers and even such a task as the pumping of water was still being done by literal horse-power in 1919. A few similar engines using petrol were appearing in the last pre-war years, but the tractor has to be dated rather from the war period itself. The revolution in the wheat plant, destined to make a field of wheat look so different by mid-century, had been initiated by Biffen's work at Cambridge and was beginning to make a difference to the reliability of yields and the quality of the product.

In bringing about these advances in technique there were two important stages, the fundamental research and the diffusion of knowledge. For the former, the nation had previously relied mainly on the Rothamsted research station, but in the 1900s Cambridge was interested in animal nutrition, besides the plant breeding noted above; Manchester and Birmingham studied agricultural zoology, and the new university college at Reading made dairying a special subject.

The new knowledge was diffused through a variety of channels. Government finance supported about a dozen agricultural colleges for intending farmers. Men going into practice as veterinary surgeons took the new scientific attitude, with its tracking of germs and pests. County Councils established advisory services, sometimes joining with the agricultural colleges to arrange demonstrations. Active in all such work was A. D. Hall, once Director of Rothamsted, a founder of the Institute of Agricultural Economics at Oxford in 1913, and ever at the elbow of the

[1] Cf. p. 128 below.

Board of Agriculture. The journalists played some part too, in a sprink-
ling of farmers' periodicals which have had long lives. Most important
of all, perhaps, were the big annual 'Shows' of the Royal Agricultural
Society and the county societies. These provided an enjoyable working
holiday for the farmer, just before he had to get busy with the harvest.
They were perhaps most effective in demonstrating the results of careful
breeding of animals and in advertising the products—new and old—
of the agricultural engineers. Possibly their influence was not always for
the best: they inevitably emphasized the items that made a good 'show',
and wealth was invested in the breeding of fine trotting horses just when
the internal-combustion engine was destroying their world.

The agricultural show, on a fine July day having a misleading air of
holiday, in a sense epitomized the state of British agriculture on the eve
of the First World War. Grain farming after its long squeeze at the end
of the nineteenth century appeared to have achieved a new balance.
Animal husbandry was doing well on meat and milk; horses, cattle, and
sheep were great attractions in the centre ring at 'the Show'. The wide
range of other products, now much more than a fringe, provided variety
along the sidewalks. The engineers, with their brightly painted gear and
the phut-phut of the little engines, were edging further in; so, less
obtrusively, were the scientists, especially in the tents of the seedsmen
and manufacturers of fertilizers and pesticides. Another element, slightly
discordant, was in the advertisements of the Canadian and Australian
migration departments, tempting away those ploughboys and cowherds
who had not already bicycled to work in the towns. Finally, there would
be a handful of youngsters, enjoying themselves at the end of their course
at the agricultural institute, and hoping they might find a good opening
to take up after the harvest.

In short, though R. E. Prothero (agriculture's historian and wartime
Minister) could write in 1912 that agriculture was 'sound and prosperous', its balance was uneasy. There was neither the stability that had
preceded the influx of overseas produce nor any sense of revolution in
technique. The depression had left its scar on the ownership of land: the
old generation of wealthy landlords, a good proportion of whom had
been in the habit of investing in land improvement, had been thinned
out, and new owners, though often very rich, had more limited views of
their responsibilities. With this change, the political influence of agriculture had declined and the farmers, though often Protectionist in their
views, had no chance against the policy of 'a free breakfast table'. The

farming unit remained unchanged, and the farmers remained stout individualists. Though the application of scientific knowledge had made some progress since 1900, on too large a proportion of the farms the practice remained fundamentally what grandfather had thought right. The older men distrusted new-fangled ways suggested by the trickle of students emerging from the agricultural colleges, and many of these young men drifted into journalism or occupations like estate agency that were ancillary to agriculture, instead of going into farming itself.

When war came, just as the harvest of 1914 was ripening, almost its only impact was to drain these young men from the colleges, the research institutes, and their offices in the country towns, into the army. For farming as for much else, the cry was 'Business as usual'. Strange as it may seem, it was not until the 1916 crops were in the barns and plans for 1917 were far advanced, that sinkings by submarines precipitated governmental action. A number of emergency measures were then taken to help the farmers: in the supply of seeds, fertilizers, and feeding-stuffs, the recruitment of labour from prisoners-of-war and 'the land girls', and co-operative employment of tractors and farm implements. More radically—and this ever after remained a sore point with the farmers—power was taken to enter on land that was inadequately cultivated. Then in 1917 a Corn Production Act guaranteed cereal prices for six years; it required the farmers in turn to pay certain minimum wage-rates. In the event the food shortages became so serious in 1917-19 that the statutory prices—and the wage-rates—were soon outrun by the market. The acreages under wheat and oats both rose by 35 per cent, though the continued absorption of men into the army put the farmers into extreme difficulty in harvesting this enlarged acreage in 1918. The concentration of effort on grain, and the more exhaustive milling of wheat for bread, made difficulties for the farmers in maintaining their livestock, and there was a big reduction in the numbers of sheep and pigs, though milk cattle were not reduced. An appreciable contribution to the nation's supply of potatoes, fruit, and vegetables came from hundreds of thousands of 'allotments', taken up by townspeople and worked in week-ends and summer evenings.

In the brief re-stocking boom that followed the end of the war (see p. 50 above) grain prices soared far above the guaranteed level. Although wages also rose, the landlords were not allowed to raise rents; in consequence the farmers' profits were greatly inflated while landlords found themselves squeezed between stable rent receipts and much higher outgoings for repairs and taxation. Many landlords were therefore disposed to sell while farmers, with money burning their pockets and politicians' promises blurring their foresight, were eager to buy their farms. An eighth of the land changed hands, and the ranks of the owner-occupiers were swollen with optimists, many of whom saddled themselves with expensive mortgages. An Agriculture Act in 1920, replacing the Corn Production Act, had seemed to promise continuance in peacetime of the support the submarine peril had evoked in 1917: the Act stipulated that four years' notice would be given of termination of the guaranteed prices. No sooner had this reached the statute book than the world-wide collapse of prices—including prices of all the main agricultural products—brought an abrupt revision of public policy. The guaranteed prices which, though much above pre-war prices, had looked so modest in 1919-20, now involved heavy subsidies from the Exchequer, just when public opinion cried out for slashing economies to lighten the burden of taxation. Perhaps the farmers' cause was lost the more easily because they had been conspicuous spenders of high profits when there was much public irritation by 'war profiteers'. At any rate, the 1920 Act was repealed before it was a year old, and the whole apparatus of price support and control was thrown overboard almost overnight. The farmers said some very rude things about 'the politicians', though the revulsion of policy—the breaking of firm commitments—no more than reflected a radical reassessment of the balance of advantage and disadvantage, by the townsmen who constituted the overwhelming majority of the British people.

Through the remainder of the 'twenties the farmers were, in the main, left to make the most they could of markets exposed to world competition. Prices of their products remained well above the immediately pre-war level, but not as much up as the general level of prices. Still less could agricultural prices bear comparison with the wage-rates men could earn in the towns and the farmers were forced—even before Parliament enacted wage regulation in 1924—to pay wages almost double those of 1914. Tenant farmers were of course helped by the failure of rents to match the general rise of prices, though this had adverse effects on the finance of land improvement. In altogether tighter position were the farmers who had borrowed some of the money to buy their farms at the fantastic prices of 1919-20. Many farms changed hands yet again, and the bankruptcy courts were busy. Products other than grain were again, as before 1914, the more profitable (or less unprofitable). Dairy farming increased in the eastern counties, with mechanical milkers becoming common and trained workers emerging from the agricultural institutes. The area under fruit trees was noticeably increasing; potatoes, too, though declining from their wartime peak of 800,000 acres, did not drop back to the pre-war level.

One innovation came to the rescue on quite a large scale in the eastern counties. On the Continent sugar-beet had been an important product for decades, though it leaned heavily on governmental help. There had been attempts in England since about 1850, but these had never attracted effective political favour and one after another had failed. The acute shortage of sugar in wartime, however, brought public opinion round in a sufficiently lasting manner, and when the economy campaigns of 1921-2 subsided, Parliament provided, by the British Sugar (Subsidy) Act of 1925, enough financial help to encourage production of the beet and manufacture of sugar. The crop soon became a popular one, especially in replacement of grain, and the acreage rose from nothing to over 300,000 in the early 1930s. A typical development of the 1920s was important in transporting the crop: the sugar-beet lorries soon became a familiar sight in the Suffolk lanes, as they converged on Bury St. Edmunds where the first and largest of the sugar factories was established.

The form of aid to sugar-beet was influenced by the 'new industry argument' which contemporary economists would concede to critics of Free Trade: a very high initial subsidy was to decline and then disappear at the end of ten years. The hope that the new industry, over its teething troubles, would then be able to stand on its own feet, was doomed to disappointment. Never a good prospect, it finally disappeared when sugar prices collapsed in the depression of 1929-32. That depression, however, had meant much else to agriculture, and had led to a piecemeal but substantial policy of support for the farmers. As part of that general policy, and no longer for cossetting a new industry, the subsidy was put on a permanent basis by the Sugar Industry (Reorganization) Act of 1936. It was a costly way of getting a quarter of the nation's sugar, but a few years later a besieged Britain thought it had been worth the price.

A dominant element in the world-wide slump of 1929-33 was the apparent glut in agricultural markets and a steep fall in agricultural prices. The British index of agricultural prices (1911-13 = 100) fell from 144 in 1929 to 112 in 1932 and 107 in 1933. The price of wheat was halved, oats fell by a third, and barley by a quarter. To large sections of an industry that had been depressed for years, this was a devastating blow. The farmers had no reserves on which to draw, many rents could scarcely be squeezed any lower, and neither law nor opinion would allow appreciable cut in wage-rates. Farms were left untenanted, and the owners had no incentive to take them in hand. Good arable land was allowed to 'tumble down' to rough pasture; routine tasks like hedging and ditching were left undone and the countryside took on a bedraggled, unkempt appearance that broke the hearts of farmers and workers who were too old to move away from it. Not least of the troubles was that there was so little for even the youngsters to move into: there was no point in flocking into towns where the unemployed stood about the streets.

This absence of opportunity for the resources agriculture no longer wanted did much towards undermining the Free Trade doctrine that had for nearly a century inhibited any continuous government intervention in support of agriculture. In that period the labour force on the farms had dropped by 700,000; the loss in agricultural produce had been more than made good, because labour had moved to other occupations where the productivity per man was higher. This net gain to National Income constituted the case for leaving the farmer exposed to competition from all over the world. Now in the early 1930s it no longer seemed possible to argue that labour lost to agriculture meant greater gain elsewhere. When, after 1933, a slow revival in industry might have revived the traditional answers to the farmers' Protectionist demands, another kind of argument crept in to help them. The English were unwilling to acknowledge that peace was in danger, but at first subconsciously and then openly they became more receptive to proposals that might safeguard food supplies in the event of war. Nevertheless, it was only reluctantly and piecemeal that the policy of free trade in food gave way to a policy of intervention in support of home agriculture. The kind of arrangement whereby support was provided for some products was coloured by the common view that the farmers were exploited by middlemen, or at least that unorganized markets left them exposed to unnecessarily low prices.

This last element in the new agricultural policy found its expression in the Agricultural Marketing Acts of 1931 and 1933, under which organized marketing schemes were evolved for a variety of products, the marketing boards being endowed with compulsory powers. The most important of these was the Milk Marketing Board, which attempted with some success to create a price system that would shield the farmers from the annual glut when richer pastures coincided with a seasonal decline in demand for milk. A feature that aroused criticism was the system of minimum retail prices, but the public was mollified by some rise in quality, and by special low prices for milk supplied to school-children and to certain groups of workpeople. The arrangements for cheap milk in schools were largely responsible for a sharpening of the population's taste for milk, a change that has become more important as those children grew up. Other factors worked in the same direction: advertisement campaigns by the Milk Marketing Board, the establishment of milk bars, and perhaps also the introduction of bottling and other improvements in the technique of distribution. Dairy farmers were also helped by regulation of imports, annual or quarterly maxima being set for imports from the main overseas sources. Protective measures for the farmers' output of meat were important from 1932, when after the Ottawa Economic Conference agreements were made with Dominion governments, and with Eire, regulating imports. A network of international organizations, such as the Empire Beef Council, was gradually evolved, and with each year the devices for support became more elaborate.

Special action was taken on wheat at an early stage. By the Wheat Act of 1932, the farmers were paid a standard price of 45s. a quarter, subject to a quantity limit (eventually raised so high as to be practically inoperative). The difference between this price and that ruling in the open market was financed by a levy on all imported wheat and flour. There was thus in effect an import duty, devoted to subsidizing the farmer, while the consumer paid a price that averaged out the high cost of home wheat and the low cost of imported wheat. Under this stimulus the wheat acreage went up again, and in the last years before the war had regained the level of the first decade of the century. This recovery was at the expense of the acreage devoted to other grains, barley and oats, and in 1938 action was taken to encourage these two crops.

In an industry as diversified as agriculture, the wide movements of prices of the various products and the piecemeal introduction of government support inevitably led to unwelcome repercussions and so to further development and elaboration of schemes for this, that, and the other product. The consumers' slow but pronounced reaction to relative price movements further complicated the situation. Cheap grain, for example, meant low costs for poultry farmers, and cheap food meant more room in the housewife's budget for luxury foods, and poultry farmers encountered a permanent increase in demand. Margarine's invasion of the butter market was turned back, and the nation's taste for milk underwent a lasting change. The tortuous efforts of the Pigs and Bacon Boards (including regulation of imports) helped, along with lower prices of feeding-stuffs, to double the home output of bacon, though here the town consumer, clinging to his preference for Danish bacon, was less obliging. When world prices rose in the later 'thirties, the boot was on the other foot, and livestock producers grumbled afresh. In 1937 they were given more permanent help by the Livestock Industry Act, and in the next year the government took further action on bacon and pigs, lamb and mutton. By this time potatoes were the only major product not subsidized in one form or another, and it had become impossible to think of this aid as being purely temporary. The National Farmers' Union could assume that the nation had been won to the general principle of support for the industry, and in the last months of peace the Union put forward a comprehensive scheme of guaranteed prices. This was still under discussion when it had to be superseded by more drastic emergency action, but it became the basis of post-war policy.

Thus the industry which in 1939 had to accept the emergency call had been shaped by centuries of traditional practice, by nearly a century of shrinkage and adjustment under the stress of exposure to developing competitors overseas, by growing variety in the nation's taste for perishable foods, by a few years of experimental government help for one product after another, and by the infiltration of engineering and science. This last had been so slow that an immense range of methods could be seen. Tractors had been creeping in for twenty years, but oxen could still be seen drawing the plough in Oxfordshire, and in 1939 there were still 650,000 horses on the farms of Britain. On small farms in Essex the flail (there called the 'stick and a half') was in use, not many miles from big farms that were among the 150 users (in 1939) of combine harvesters. It was difficult to imagine that technical practice was about to develop at headlong pace, that within another twenty years the horse would have become merely a Saturday morning mount for the farmer's daughter and that agriculture would be among the industries with the highest ratios of capital to labour.

8

The Preface to the Welfare State

IN THE DECADES AROUND 1900 the great majority of Englishmen—
and a considerable proportion of the women as well—won a living by
entering into contracts of service. Half the occupied population were in
employments where the processes had been radically changed during
the Industrial Revolution, and half of this half were in 'industrial'
employment. For most people the ways in which they spent their working hours, and the amount and security of the income they drew from
their work, were dependent on the decisions of their employers. The
weekly contract of service had become almost universal, and its insecurity, with the worker's consequent inferiority in bargaining power,
was emphasized by the frequency of unemployment. There were always
some employers who were willing to incur avoidable losses rather than
turn away the workpeople who were dependent on them, but few could
afford such paternalism for long, and the harshness of competition in
the market more generally drove employers to regard the week's notice
as enforceable at any time. Before 1940 there was no real diminution in
the employee's insecurity, but from two sources there was pressure
towards improvement in the conditions at the workplace, hours of work,
and wage-rates, and towards alleviation of distress when earnings failed.
The more spectacular of these sources of pressure was the growing
power of trade unions, whose attitude was moulded by the worker's
sensitiveness to insecurity above all else. The other, less fertile in
historical incident but continuously and insistently at work, was a change
in political attitudes towards poverty and the living conditions of the less
fortunate.

The change in attitude began more as a facet of religious practice
than as the outcome of any revolution of political thought. Within the

E

Established Church in the earlier decades of the nineteenth century, practice had been enlivened by the Evangelical and Tractarian movements, and out of this more vital atmosphere more practical interest in the worldly distresses and discomforts of others had grown. Other religious sects, notably the Society of Friends, increasingly attached importance to good works among one's neighbours, and the desire to do good led (and this was much in the spirit of the time) to uncovering of the facts of poverty and distress. As more became known, people became more conscious of responsibility to help, and in the second half of the century the proliferation of philanthropic bodies was such as to lead, after 1869, to the growth of Charity Organization societies to systematize voluntary aid and prevent overlapping with the relief provided by the Poor Law Guardians. In both the ancient universities this change of heart was revealed in a new interest and activity in the slums of great cities: Toynbee Hall (1884), Cambridge House, and other 'Settlements' were established in the East End of London, as places where university men, drawn exclusively from the upper classes, could at once learn 'how the other half lived' and do something to make life more tolerable in this world and incidentally save a few souls for the next. At the same time a wealthy shipowner, Charles Booth, was making his *Survey of Life and Labour in London* (published 1891-1903) which provided a generation of radical reformers with information to weight their arguments. The studies of the Fabian Socialists were of the same kind and had similar influence: Marxian theories had little impact on nineteenth-century England, but there was a breaking down of resistance to State intervention in economic affairs, and the reformers presented their proposals as administrative measures for dealing with widely admitted evils, rather than as an overturning of the social system. From the beginning of the twentieth century this source of radical pressure became a more serious political force through its association with trade unionism to form the Labour Party. This third party effectively entered parliamentary politics in the 1906 General Election; its first role was as a supporter of a strong Liberal Government whose measures of social and economic reform reflected the turn taken by opinion twenty years earlier. In 1924 and again in 1929 the Labour Party was strong enough to form a minority government, but it was still, and it remained throughout this period, substantially dependent on trade-union support.

This political success of the trade-union movement was a novelty of the decades after 1880. In mid-Victorian England trade unionism had been confined almost entirely to skilled workers, the aims of the individual unions (many of them very small bodies) were confined to protection of the narrow interests of their own members, and there had been more hostility than alliance between one union and another. This meant in practice that the unions bargained with employers on questions of wages, hours, and conditions of work for themselves, occasionally using the strike weapon in assertion of their bargaining power; they took a strong line on demarcation and apprenticeship questions, in order to restrict the supply of labour in their craft; and they used rough-and-ready systems of mutual insurance to provide for their members in sickness and other distress. In effect they were making, for their own members, the best they could of the operation of 'the laws of supply and demand' which they themselves, as well as the employers and independent observers, accepted as the rulers of the economic system. Seen as an attitude of self-help, this attitude in the trade unions of the 'sixties and 'seventies appealed to the spirit of the times, and helped to persuade employers to accept the unions as facts of life. This acceptance showed itself in the establishment, in the 'sixties and 'seventies, of conciliation boards or other continuous joint organizations of employers and employed, for dealing with industrial disputes. Some of these conciliation boards—in the boot and shoe industry and in the iron and steel industry for example—were highly successful; others depended on the enthusiasm and abilities of one or two individuals and fizzled out after a few years of useful activity. The participation of the trade unions in continuous collective bargaining of this kind did much to win their acceptance by public opinion as a respectable part of an ordered society.

This was not the whole story; the generalized picture just given glosses over the occasional upsurge of more revolutionary ideas, more violent conflicts, and an underlying bitterness that in some trades and places meant that industrial peace depended on the worker's fear of unemployment rather than on any acceptance of the mutual interest of employer and employed in the working of the economic system. This darker current was apt to come to the surface in bad times, and in the patch of heavy unemployment in 1886 there were some ugly scenes. It was, however, in the good years at the end of this decade that the aspect of industrial relations and trade-union development was abruptly and irrevocably changed. The turning-point is marked by two great strikes and one victory without a strike, in trades where unionism had been virtually non-existent. In 1888 the London match-girls struck; in 1889, the

London dockers paralysed the port for five weeks and won the 6*d*.-an-hour wage-rate ('the dockers' tanner'); and in 1889 the gas-workers won, without a strike, the 8-hours' day in replacement of the previous 12-hours' day. These successes by workers not previously organized encouraged the rise of massive trade unions, such as the Gasworkers' and General Labourers' Union, among unskilled workers, and the total membership of trade unions jumped from about one million in the 1880s to a million and a half in the early 1890s and to two millions in 1900. The new unions were more militant than the older unions of skilled men, whose 'Friendly Society obsession' they criticized as inadequate. They refused to acknowledge any inevitability in existing levels of wages, and showed great interest in political action for improvement in the position of the workers.

The spectacle of this new militant trade unionism, the industrial friction and disputes in which the new unions were born, and the new interest thoughtful people had found in labour matters, led to the appointment in 1891 of a Royal Commission on Labour. This body spent two years collecting information and opinions. It addressed itself particularly to the question of government intervention in industrial disputes. It surveyed the experience of the conciliation boards which seemed to have been doing very well without any legislative action. The intervention of an independent body seemed often to be helpful, and the Commission thought that a government department could serve a useful purpose in this way, without any need to force the parties to accept arbitration. The Board of Trade had for some time been acting upon occasion as a mediator, and had sometimes helped the parties in a dispute to find an arbitrator; and in 1893, while the Commission was sitting, the Board had established within itself a separate Labour Department. By the Conciliation Act of 1896 Parliament explicitly recognized the power of the Board of Trade to intervene in industrial disputes, and in the following twenty years its Labour Department won for itself, by its wise and forthright exercise of this power, quite extraordinarily high prestige, a reputation that was maintained when in 1917 the Labour Department of the Board of Trade was transformed into the Ministry of Labour.

The main lines of Factory legislation, in the sense of regulation of physical conditions at the workplace and of hours of work, and restriction of the employment of women and children, had already been laid down before 1880; and nearly half a century of experience had been gained by the Factory Inspectorate charged with the enforcement of these laws. In the period between 1880 and 1914 there was no revolutionary extension of these laws, but there was a characteristic probing of conditions in some of the smaller occupations which had escaped attention when Parliament was busy legislating on coal-mines, cotton mills, and other major employments. There were official inquiries, for example, into conditions in the match factories, in fish-curing, and in laundries; and Parliament woke up to the fact that the long hours shops were open implied intolerably long hours for employees, among them a high proportion of young people. The revelation—by Charles Booth and others—of conditions in the sweated labour industries, leading (as is described below) to minimum-wage legislation, emphasized the need for extending the Factory Acts to cover industries and workplaces that had escaped the earlier legislation.

Throughout the period one of the chief driving forces behind reform was the exposure of facts by the Factory Inspectors. Resistance continued to come from people (sometimes the workers themselves) who argued that opportunities for earning a living would be destroyed by increasing State prohibitions on this and that, but accumulating experience, systematic investigation, and the attitude of those employers who believed that productivity could be raised by improved conditions—all these factors gave weight to the arguments for extension of the Acts. The emphasis throughout was on administrative measures to deal with specific evils, rather than any doctrinaire development of a logical code. In 1893 two women Factory Inspectors were appointed for the first time; further development of the Inspectorate came in 1898, and by 1910 medical, engineering, and other specialists, besides eighteen women, were included in the team. The Act of 1891 brought the local authorities into the enforcement of the law, though it was not until another Act had been passed, in 1895, that really widespread activity by local authorities became an important adjunct to the work of the Inspectorate. This was important, because the Acts of 1891 and 1895 had greatly extended the number of workplaces subject to this kind of regulation; particularly, sanitary arrangements and physical conditions in the workplaces were regulated in much greater detail than before. Special requirements were imposed where dangerous or unhealthy processes were employed. A consolidating Act, the Factory and Workshop Act of 1901, tidied up what had become a very complex body of law, besides remedying deficiencies of detail exposed by the experience of the Inspectorate and by the more lively and probing public interest now shown in these problems. The laundries were left in anomalous freedom until 1907, when another Act subjected them to most of the restrictions common to other workplaces.

Public heart-searching was perhaps the most important force behind the enactment of the Employment of Children Act in 1903. A careful investigation was made into the employment of children—estimated at 200,000 including 22,000 under 10—in street-trading, agriculture, and certain other occupations. The Act prohibited the employment of children in any occupation likely to be injurious to their physical health and condition or their education; employment in street-trading under the age of 11 was prohibited, and hours of any employment were restricted. Another special class of workers was the seamen; they were protected by the Merchant Shipping Acts of 1894 and 1906, prescribing minimum standards of water and food supplies, and a variety of other matters affecting their welfare and health.

The State was thus taking continually more care to protect employees from bad conditions at their places of work. If, in spite of all that could reasonably be done to protect him, he suffered damage in the course of his work, the worker had substantially no remedy before 1897. He could, in theory, bring an action against his employer, but even if he could afford the cost of litigation his rights were so hedged about as to be non-existent in practice. In 1897, by the Workmen's Compensation Act, Parliament introduced the principle that the employer must compensate an injured workman (or dependants if the workman was killed), even if there was no wrongful act or omission on the part of the employer or of anyone employed by him. Early experience under the Act was examined by a Committee in 1903, and again in 1919; legislation in 1906, 1923, and 1925 implemented many consequential recommendations, making the workman's protection more complete.

Outside the range of actual legislation, the trade-union movement had in 1891 won a notable advance for the principle of the standard wage when the House of Commons first adopted a 'Fair Wages Resolution'. This required all government contractors to pay the wage-rates standard in the district, so preventing employers from undercutting their competitors' prices for government work by paying less than standard rates. The resolution was quickly followed by many local government authorities. A revised form was adopted by the House of Commons in 1909 and rapidly became common form for all contracts placed by public authorities; it required all government contractors and sub-contractors to pay rates of wages and to observe hours of labour not less favourable than those commonly adopted by employers generally, having regard to the nature of the work and the district in which it had to be carried out. Though not taking the form of an Act of Parliament this Fair Wages Resolution has equal force since government departments must observe the requirements of the House of Commons which votes the money to pay for the work done by government contractors. In effect it has meant that government contractors pay at least trade-union rates to all their employees, since it is not practicable to pay one rate for work for a government contract while paying another rate for work for other customers.

The wage question on which public opinion was most deeply stirred at this time was, however, that of 'sweated labour', as the phrase went. There were some trades in which, as now became generally known, workers, sometimes but not always women, sometimes but not always in their own homes, were working for wages so low that no one could suppose they would allow the workers a tolerable existence. From 1885 onwards the public conscience was increasingly troubled by these black spots, especially of the chain-makers at Cradley Heath, lace-makers, box-makers, and sections of the clothing trades in the East End of London. In 1890 a Select Committee of the House of Lords made some inquiry, and during the following years various private bills were brought before Parliament though without success. In 1906 agitation became more forceful, with the formation of the Anti-Sweating League; in 1907 and 1908 Select Committees on Home Work investigated the problem more thoroughly and finally broke down resistance to statutory minimum wages. The Trade Boards Act of 1909 followed the main lines of the Report of the 1908 Committee. It specified four trades, and required the government to add to the list any other appropriate cases, where the wage-rate was 'exceptionally low as compared with that in other employments'. For each of these trades a Trade Board was established, consisting of equal numbers of employers' and employees' representatives with a few independent members. Each Trade Board was required to fix minimum rates of wages to be paid to all workers in the trade. Enforcement could be either by criminal prosecution of the employer or by civil proceedings initiated by underpaid workers (there was at least one such civil case); and government inspectors were to be appointed. To the four trades (chain-making and the others mentioned above) specified in the Act, four others had been added by 1915; in these eight trades half a million workers were employed. The minimum rates fixed by the Boards were (as public opinion required) above those previously paid, though not by a wide margin. The dire consequences foretold by doctrinaire opponents did not materialize, and the better employers were glad enough of statutory protection against wage-cutting competitors. The higher earnings, though still pitifully low, made the workers more efficient and proved unfounded the fears of higher costs that would check the demand for labour.

Before the Trade Boards Act had introduced statutory minimum wages for the lowest paid, the average full-time earnings for men, skilled and unskilled, high-paid and low-paid industrial occupations taken together, had been shown in the first Census of Production (1906) to be 28s. 6d. for men and 14s. 2d. for women. Twenty years earlier the figure would have been at least 10 per cent lower; the rise continued throughout the pre-war period, bringing the 1914 average for men perhaps to 30s. The rise in money-wage rates, however, barely offset the rise in the cost of living, so little rise in living standards was possible except for those, such as the Lancashire cotton operatives, whose wages were rising more rapidly than the average. In the less prosperous parts of the country—in corn-growing East Anglia, for example, where the farm labourer's wage was just creeping up to 12s. or 12s. 6d., and in the coalfields—there was a decided sense of belt-tightening as prices rose in the new century. Women in domestic service, 'living-in' and so escaping the impact of rising food prices, did better, their cash wages being £20-£25 a year, nearly as much as was paid to women in industry who lacked the advantage of board and lodging; but the lack of freedom in domestic service was irksome, and the relatively good remuneration failed to draw as many girls as the employers would have liked. The money wage is not everything, even when allowance is made for the measured changes in the cost of living; there were other widespread and important changes operating to affect material welfare, some one way and some the other, although they cannot be quantified. On the one side was a serious deterioration in nutritional standards due to the popularization of condensed milk and to the replacement of stone-ground flour by roller-ground flour; these changes led to great vitamin deficiencies, so that a whole generation of children were exceptionally prone to rickets, bad teeth, and anaemia. On the other side of the account was the decline in drunkenness, both of men and women. This decline implied an appreciable reduction of wastage of the family's income; it was a slow decline between 1900 and 1914, but even in these years the Saturday football match, the bicycle and the bus were beginning to rival drunkenness, as Professor Phelps Brown has remarked, as 'the quickest way out of Manchester'.

These were circumstances affecting those who were fortunate enough to be in continuous employment, but the really distressing poverty was not due to lowness of wages. The new sensitiveness of English society to the problems of poverty, and the more scientific approach to them, were apparent in the work of the Royal Commission on the Poor Laws, appointed in 1905 and reporting in 1909. Fabian Socialists, led by Sidney and Beatrice Webb, shaped the Minority Report, the classic example of a Minority Report that outshone and outlived a Majority Report. The approach of the Minority was an insistence on analysis of the diverse causes of poverty and the recommendation that the State should tackle each part of the problem by tackling the relevant cause. Some people were destitute because opportunities for employment were insufficient; others had grown too old for work; others were ill; and only relatively few were poor because they preferred a tramp's life to regular employment. The study of unemployment as a major cause of poverty was greatly advanced at this time by the publication (1909) of *Unemployment: a Problem of Industry*, by W. H. Beveridge (later Lord Beveridge), a book that at once became the standard work on the subject. Beveridge showed how the problem of unemployment should be regarded as a group of problems. There was unemployment due to secular decline in demand for labour in particular occupations (which might be due either to failure of demand for the product or to replacement of handicraft by machine methods); there were cyclical depressions of trade alternating with the good years, and causing unemployment most heavily in industries producing capital goods; there was seasonal unemployment; and there was unemployment due to excessive labour supply in occupations where employment was casual. There was accordingly, in Beveridge's view (and this has been followed by all later authorities), no single cure for unemployment. Each kind of unemployment called for separate treatment: the secular decline in demand must be met by helping people to find new niches in the industrial world, the cyclical unemployment must be tackled by seeking a preventive of the trade cycle, seasonal unemployment called both for more mobility of labour and for efforts to smooth the flow of production over the year, and casual unemployment could be reduced only by altering the methods of engaging labour at the docks and such places. A many-sided assault on this complex of problems appeared to be the best way of dealing with, by removing at the roots, a substantial part of the destitution that was now no longer accepted as part of the divine order of things. A large part of British economic and social policy during the following sixty years springs from this new analytical approach to the phenomenon of poverty among plenty.

Though every part of the analysis at once had an impact on thought and gradually came to shape the beginnings of the Welfare State, the immediate steps were comparatively minor, though radical enough in their nature. The old-age pension, non-contributory, did not have to await the reports of the Poor Law Commission; it was established by Act of Parliament in 1908. By providing 5s. a week for any person from the age of 70 it at once removed a large number from the scope of the Poor Law and brought happiness to thousands of others who, approaching old age, had been dreading resort to the relieving officer if not to the workhouse itself. 'God bless Lloyd George', said the old people, of the Minister responsible for the Bill, though more fairly they should have named Asquith. Amazingly swift action came on one recommendation common to both the Majority and Minority Reports of the Poor Law Commission. This was the establishment of Labour Exchanges, for helping the able-bodied unemployed to find other jobs. The Act giving the necessary power to the Labour Department was passed in 1909 and the first Exchanges were opened in February 1910, Beveridge himself being one of the civil servants whose energy gave such rapid effect to Winston Churchill's Act. The third of the early steps (they were never viewed as a single programme, although they sprang from a single intellectual and political source) was Lloyd George's National Insurance Act of 1911, establishing a system of insurance against sickness, compulsory for most employed people, and a partial system of unemployment insurance. The health insurance part of the scheme, carried by Lloyd George in the teeth of strong opposition, was in the event one of the greatest triumphs of the nation's administrative machine. Both parts of the scheme (sickness and unemployment insurance) embodied the principle of contributions by employer, employee, and the Exchequer; it also built on and made full administrative use of the experience of the Friendly Societies and of trade unions which had been acting as Friendly Societies in their 'benefit' systems. Finally (in terms of what was done before the 1914 war), a start was made on the problem of casual labour at the docks. Work at the docks was run on the basis of engagement in haphazard fashion at the dock gates, for half a day at a time. This resulted in the docks being surrounded by thousands of men, some of them almost unemployable, who waited on the chance of catching the foreman's eye, though there was never any possibility that all— or even most—of them could be employed continuously. At Liverpool in 1912, and in London after the war, a system of registration of dock workers was introduced, employment being confined to men who could, by reference to their experience and capacity, establish some claim to be regarded as regular workers. At the outset it was in fairness necessary to register far more than could be continuously employed, but some reduction in the pool of idle labour was effected at once and further gradual reduction was possible in course of time. Decasualization, as this process was called, did not directly reduce unemployment, but by limiting the chance of engagement to fewer men, it drove thousands of others through the Labour Exchanges into other avenues of employment.

In two other important directions—housing and education—the Welfare State was being foreshadowed by government intervention in the second half of the nineteenth century; in both, there was noticeable acceleration in the first years of the twentieth century. In housing, the first intervention had been of a negative kind, in the sanitary legislation arising as much from the scientists' understanding of disease as from any tenderness towards the working classes. By the 'seventies, however, a more positive attitude was developing; housing began to be regarded as 'the root problem of social reform' and dedicated men and women— Octavia Hill chief among them—began to tackle it. In 1874-5 Parliament authorized local authorities to undertake the re-housing of some of those living in the worst conditions. A Royal Commission Report in 1885 was followed by a series of Acts strengthening the powers of local authorities, especially by giving them the power of compulsory purchase. Private organizations, such as the Peabody Trust which built great blocks of working-class tenements in the East End of London, were more active than local authorities in providing new dwellings, but the local authorities became increasingly active, especially after 1909, in making houses 'fit for human habitation'. Before 1914 well over 100,000 of the $5\frac{1}{2}$ million working-class houses had been thus renovated, though no more than 15,000 had actually been erected by local authorities. The year 1909 had been a landmark, in that the Act of that year, besides stirring up the local authorities in their housing activities, was not just a housing Act but a Housing and Town Planning Act. People had begun to discuss town-planning seriously before 1900; there had been two notable efforts by industrialists, at Port Sunlight since 1887 and at Bournville since 1895. In 1898 Ebenezer Howard's book *Garden Cities of To-morrow* had appeared; it inspired Letchworth (1903) and after the war Welwyn Garden City. In the rural districts practically nothing was done; but in the towns the movement for better housing and better planning was just getting up steam when a halt was called by the war of 1914-18. When that was over, the scarcity due to five years without new houses and a great increase in the number of families, sharpened by the demand for 'homes fit for heroes', forced the government and local authorities to enter the business of house-building and letting on a massive scale.

In 1870 less than half the children in the country attended any school, but Forster's Education Act in that year had established School Boards which by 1890 had more or less filled the gaps in the provision of elementary education, and the Boards were able to insist on attendance by all up to the age of 11 or 12. In 1890 some small provision of finance— referred to as 'the whiskey money'[1]—was made for technical education, in which Britain was just becoming sensitive to her backwardness as compared with Germany and other countries; in the following year all elementary education became free. The first provision for secondary education was by the Balfour Government's Act of 1902, but in large sections of the country this got off to a very slow start. The Act of 1902 also sought to improve elementary education by putting the Board schools and the 'voluntary' (mostly Church of England) schools on the same footing; this stirred up the last great outburst of religious sectarianism in British politics and thus, perversely enough, this effort in social legislation became one of the major factors that swept the Conservatives from office and brought in the Liberals in 1906. The new government acted quickly on a report on the physical condition of the schoolchildren: first by authorizing local authorities to provide meals, and then by compelling them to appoint school medical officers. The ensuing medical inspections were sometimes perfunctory, but the facts they brought to light helped to make the nation dimly aware of the damage that was being done by the drop in nutritional standards.

While the Liberal Government was thus laying the foundations of the

---

[1] 'The whiskey money' was derived from part of a tax on spirits set aside for the fostering of technical education.

Welfare State, the trade-union movement was increasing its pressure on employers, and industrial conflict rose to a fresh peak in the years 1910–13. One of the main trouble-spots was on the railways, then owned by joint-stock companies which in general resisted the claims of trade unions to represent the men. In the law courts trade unionism had, as a result of one railway dispute (the Taff Vale case), suffered a severe setback, when a railwaymen's union was held liable to pay damages to the company whose men had struck. This decision, always doubtful law, was reversed by Act of Parliament in 1906. In 1907 the Amalgamated Railway Servants, with the support of the government, won from the companies the principle that wages should be settled by boards of conciliation and arbitration; again in 1911 the government coerced the employers into a settlement of a national railway strike, and from that date onwards the railway unions were among the most powerful in the country. The change in the atmosphere of the determination of wages had also been seen in unusually widespread resistance to wage-cuts in the sharp depression of 1908: hitherto the workers had tended fatalistically to accept some wage-cutting as the inevitable order of events in a spell of bad trade, but employers now met an altogether firmer front.

The strife of 1910–13 involved by no means all sections of wage-earners or even of industrial wage-earners. Most of it was confined to the coal-mines, the railways, and a few other trades where unions had been weak, but even so, the total of working days lost in disputes rose to new heights. Over the previous twenty years, time lost in disputes had averaged about 7 million working days (less than one day per worker), but 1912 set the pre-war record with the loss of nearly 41 million days, an average of four days for every worker in the country. This was the year of the most complete stoppage of coal-mining the country had yet known; only after the introduction of the Miners Minimum Wage Act did the five-weeks' stoppage break up. Under this Act district conferences were to negotiate minimum rates for each district, with official arbitration as a last resort. This was an extreme case of government intervention, but there were many less spectacular interventions, and it became almost common form for the Board of Trade's Labour Department, and sometimes Ministers themselves, to take some initiative when the nation was threatened with any uncomfortable stoppage. In 1911 the government had tried a general remedy, in the shape of an 'Industrial Council' to inquire into industrial disputes. This consisted of thirteen representatives of workers and thirteen of employers and, as Chairman,

Sir George Askwith, who (not to be confused with the Prime Minister, Asquith) was Chief Industrial Commissioner in the Labour Department. Like many other attempts in many countries, this attempt at generality proved disappointing; it ceased to exist after two years, most of its real work having been done by Askwith himself. More generally, the episode may be said to have won for a wider range of workers the right to bargain through their trade unions, sometimes on a national scale, and to have emphasized the public interest in the ventilation of the rights and wrongs of any industrial dispute that threatened to cause widespread inconvenience.

The war of 1914-18 inevitably brought further governmental intervention in the wage-fixing processes and, partly because of this, some more lasting growth of the habit of negotiation on a national scale by permanent organizations both of employers and of workers. The development of governmental machinery took an odd form, growing unexpectedly out of the activity of a 'Committee on Production in Engineering and Shipbuilding Establishments' which the government set up in February 1915 for more general purposes relating to war production. The most urgent problems in the industries under pressure happened to be labour problems, and so the Committee went into action as a wage-fixing body. Its power to act in this manner was confirmed and extended by the Munitions of War Act in July 1915; under this Act the wage-awards of the Committee were to be binding. Despite the title of the Act, the powers were extended far beyond the munitions industries; the Committee's own label was habitually shortened to 'Committee on Production', and in typically English fashion the nation found itself accepting for a wide range of occupations compulsory arbitration by a body called the Committee on Production acting under legislation ostensibly referring to munitions of war. Under wartime conditions, with public opinion strongly behind the government, enforcement of the Committee's awards presented no great difficulty. As the war progressed, the Committee found itself busy also with other questions on which organized labour was apt to hold strong views: particularly there were questions of partial replacement of skilled by unskilled men ('dilution of labour') and of the employment of women to do work formerly the preserve of men. Though there were some awkward disputes from time to time, the work of the Committee went fairly smoothly, especially after increases in wages more or less automatically reflected rises in the cost of living.

Wartime circumstances also gave some impetus to official interest, and employers' interest, in industrial welfare. The employment of women for unaccustomed tasks and in unaccustomed places, the general effort to make the most of industry's depleted labour force, and perhaps indirectly the realization, coming from medical examination of recruits for the Armed Forces, that the nation had been too careless of the physical condition of its manpower, all made for more thought and care for the industrial environment of those on whom war supplies most directly depended. Through the greater part of the war a very important official body, the Health of Munition Workers Committee, was active in ascertaining the facts and investigating and promoting possibilities for improved conditions at the workplace. Its success led after the war to the foundation of the Industrial Fatigue Research Board, more or less a government institution but including employers' and workers' representation, for continuing the work of the Committee. Similar considerations had influenced the shape and the efficiency of a new Factories Act in 1916, which extended far beyond factories, including even the police force. Under this Act many 'Welfare Orders' were made regarding meals, drinking water, protective clothing, ambulance services, seats in workrooms, washing facilities, etc. Further regulations were also made under the 'dangerous trades clauses' of the 1901 Factories and Workshops Act.

Problems in the munitions industries in 1916 prompted the extension of the unemployment insurance part of the Act of 1911 to cover all munitions workers and those in the metal, chemical, and other industries. Temporary measures for universal unemployment relief were necessary to cover the dislocation immediately after the war, and then in November 1920 the insurance scheme was put on a permanent footing, to cover all manual workers (except in agriculture) and most low-paid white-collar workers. The insurance principle—whereby benefit depended on previous contributions—was maintained, but the need to deal with continuous unemployment of large numbers caused this principle to be whittled away. Successive governments clung to the word 'insurance', but this came to mean no more than that unemployment pay was partly financed by a tax on employment. This unemployment pay included allowances for dependents; such allowances did not feature in the health insurance scheme but were accepted as the only way of keeping down the cost of relieving the unemployed consistently with allowing tolerable subsistence for their families. Incidentally, these allowances helped to accustom people to the idea that recognition of family needs should be included in the kind of comprehensive 'social security' system towards which opinion was moving.

After the war, public opinion was always solidly behind extended application of the principles of 'the Factory Acts' in the light of experience, but it was not until 1937 that there was new legislation embracing the great range of detailed reforms whose desirability had become apparent. When at last Parliament found time, the task was done thoroughly, and in a manner that was to become typical of legislation after 1945. Before the Bill went to Parliament there was consultation between the officials, the Factory Inspectorate, the employers' associations, and the trade unions; it was to an exceptional degree a measure agreed in detail by those most concerned. This Factories Act of 1937 contains 160 sections, arranged in fourteen Parts: the Parts deal with health, safety, welfare, accidents, industrial diseases, employment of women and young persons, homework, notification of piece-rates, etc., and administration. It was an extraordinarily detailed measure, and the inspectorate, though now numbered in hundreds instead of tens, could not possibly enforce it were it not for the full support of public opinion and the active interest of both employers' organizations and trade unions.

When, for more energetic prosecution of the First World War, the trade unions had accepted dilution of labour, the government had promised that such concessions, which were contrary to the protectionist spirit of the skilled men's unions, should be swept away when the needs of war had been satisfied. The promise was implemented by the Restoration of Pre-War Practices Act in 1919. The powers of the Committee on Production lapsed. There was, however, a widespread feeling on both sides in industry that industrial relations ought not to be left to drift back into the militant atmosphere of 1910-13. Following the recommendations of the Whitley Committee, Joint Industrial Councils were established in seventy-three industries. These were intended to be wider than the conciliation boards that had been a feature of the more peaceful industries before the war; they were national rather than local, and they were intended to deal with a wider range of problems. In the event, a few of these Councils settled wages, working conditions, and hours, and exceptionally they organized technical education and promoted industrial research; but many were quite ineffective, and their number had dwindled to fifty in 1925. Despite a National Industrial Conference in 1919, the good intentions of the 'reconstruction' phase to some extent evaporated. When the post-war boom collapsed, prices tumbled, firms faced cancellation of orders, and wage-cutting became general. Eventually the wage-increases of the war period were reversed to the extent of about three-fifths; the rapid fall in the cost of living reconciled people to much of this fall in wages, but not before—in 1921—there had been prolonged strikes, most damagingly in the coal industry.

The notion that some regular wage-fixing machinery was universally desirable had permanently advanced, however. This showed in the extension of the Trade Boards Act beyond its original intention of covering only the 'sweated labour' spots. By an amending Act of 1918, the Ministry of Labour was empowered to establish a Trade Board where no adequate wage-fixing machinery existed, though still having regard to the rates of wages prevailing. Trade Boards were then set up thick and fast, bringing the total trades covered to thirty-five, employing $1\frac{1}{2}$ million people, by the end of 1921. The principle of determination by a wages board was extended to the railways when the Railways Act of 1921 established, on Trade Board lines but without compulsory powers, the National Wages Board for Railways. For the three-quarters of a million in agriculture the Agricultural Wages (Regulation) Act of 1924 established county wages committees, with a national board to approve the rates proposed by the county committees. The wages were to be 'adequate to promote efficiency, and to enable a man in an ordinary case to maintain himself and his family in accordance with such standard of comfort as may be reasonable in relation to the nature of his occupation'. The minimum wage-rates which the Committees regarded as meeting these requirements were about 25s. a week. After this date, governments lost what little enthusiasm they had had for wage-fixing machinery, and long arguments about bringing the catering trades under a Trade Board were inconclusive.

In one matter the workers succeeded in permanently holding an improvement won in the immediately post-war phase. Back in the 1870s most important trades had settled down to a working week of 54 or $54\frac{1}{2}$ hours. The Factory Act of 1901 set a maximum of 60 for non-textile factories and workshops; for the textile industries, $55\frac{1}{2}$ was the legal maximum. In common practice there was little change until 1914, though rather shorter weeks—48 to 53 hours—were gradually spreading, especially in engineering. For coal-mines a statutory daily maximum of 8 hours underground was fixed in 1908. Shop hours were usually very long, especially on Fridays and Saturdays when the shops were open until 8, 9, or 10 p.m. and shop assistants were expected to clear up after the shop was shut. Parliament did not make up its mind to regulate this kind of business until 1912, when maximum hours of work were fixed at 74 a week (including mealtimes) and the early closing day was made obligatory. During the war, largely under government influence, much attention was given to the relation between hours of work and productivity, and this helped to make employers, and public opinion generally, quick to accept in 1919-20 trade unions' demands for a shorter working week. A working week of $47\frac{1}{2}$ or 48 hours then became the standard in the more organized industries, and a slightly longer week in less organized trades. The week-end henceforth normally began at mid-day on Saturday, and employees who had to work in the week-end, because of continuous processes such as furnace work in metal or chemical industries, or in public utilities, were now usually paid higher rates as well as having alternative days off. Except in the coal-mines, there was hardly any further change in standard hours of work between 1920 and 1940. But trade unions were taking a firmer line on all sorts of questions of overtime; employers found themselves having to fall in with standard patterns of overtime conditions, these sometimes being laid down in national agreements with the unions. The Agricultural Wages Act of 1924 conformed with the trend: while not fixing any maximum hours of work, it provided for the fixing of overtime rates, and for a weekly half-holiday where reasonably practicable.

Although steady pressure from trade unions, aided by a continuing movement of public opinion, was able to win concessions on such questions as overtime pay, the general shortening of hours in 1919-20 was the unions' last major victory in these decades. The unions' exceptional strength in the post-war boom proved as fleeting as the boom itself. From $2\frac{1}{2}$ millions in 1910 their membership had risen to 4,135,000 in 1913 and then leapt to 8,346,000 in 1920. Then came the black years of 1921, when 86 million working days were lost in strikes against the tide of falling prices and empty order books, and 1922, when unemployment rose above 20 per cent. And the 'twenties remained to the end a difficult decade—it included in 1926 a General Strike and a long coal strike that failed—and trade-union membership dwindled to 5 millions and less. After a further bout of deflation the figure was down to 4,389,000 in 1933. Some strongly organized industries—coal, cotton, and the railways—were employing fewer people than in 1920, while the growing

numbers in retailing and other 'services' and in the new light-manu-
facturing industries were not so easily organized. The shift of working
population to the Midlands, and especially to London and the south,
where unionism was much weaker, also had something to do with declining membership. But there were some 'growing spots' for unionism all
the time, notably among public servants and more generally among
women, and after 1933, with growing hold in new industries (the motor
industry among them) total membership reached 6,300,000 on the eve
of war. This still left twice as many employed people outside the movement. Internally also the movement had its weaknesses: though a few
unions could count their members in hundreds of thousands, there
were hundreds of tiny ones with little power, less influence, and many
mutual jealousies. The shrinkage of the great export industries of the
pre-1914 period had inflicted a great defeat on the trade-union movement for, besides cutting the numbers employed in the most unionized
industries, the market conditions had opened up, against all the resistance the unions could muster, a great gap between wage-rates in different industries. By 1925 this gap between the 'sheltered industries'
(those not facing foreign competition) and the 'unsheltered' was already
uncomfortably large: for the skilled man, 73s. against 58s., and for the
unskilled 50s. against 45s. The gap became larger still in the early 'thirties.
Moreover, comparison of wage-rates understates the real difference, for
the rate of promotion from unskilled to skilled slows down in a shrinking
industry; in Lancashire particularly, men of 30 and 35 were still doing
jobs (and receiving the wage-rates) that they would, before 1914, have
left behind in their early 'twenties.

Badly as the leaders of the trade-union movement felt about this distortion of the country's wage-structure, they felt even worse about the
mass unemployment in the depressed areas, which lay behind the distortion of the wage-structure; and it was this mass unemployment that
bit most deeply into the minds of the rank and file of the trade unions
and of millions outside the movement. It was this unemployment that
maintained the job-protection demarcation rules as fetishes of the trade-
union officials; and restriction of hours, like the agitation for more
holidays and early retirements, was supported by work-spreading arguments. Most of all, a whole generation grew up, inside and outside the
unions, that was determined through the years after 1945 to give top
priority in economic policy to the aim of Full Employment. For nearly
all those in a place of work, Parliament had by now assured reasonable

physical surroundings, and Parliament and the trade unions between them were protecting most of the employed from ruthless exploitation. Parliament had also taken radical steps to ensure that those unable to earn a living should not have to choose between starvation and the Poor Law. In these ways, six decades had seen great change, but by the end of the 'thirties this was not enough: the Englishman, sickened by the problem of the Depressed Areas, was now demanding that there should be enough work for every able-bodied adult to earn his living. In 1939 neither the sophisticated nor the man-in-the-street had any clear view as to how this 'full employment' was to be achieved. Even less was there any desire to find the solution, as Britain did, by plunging into total war.

9
Saving and Investment

MEN PROVIDE THEMSELVES with the consumable goods and services they want by working with natural resources and accumulated man-made equipment. In this sense, the standard of living ultimately depends on the three basic 'factors of production'—land (natural resources), labour (work of all kinds), and capital (man-made equipment, in the broadest sense), and on how effectively these resources are put to use to satisfy men's requirements. Changes in the availability of these factors of production, in the intensity with which they are used, in the nature of the goods desired, and in man's ingenuity in making them, are the causes of changes in the standard of living; if the view is restricted (as in this book) to a single country, the terms on which exports and imports are traded are further critical determinants of the standard of living. In earlier chapters something has been said on the supply and conditions of labour, the nation's foreign trade, fluctuations in economic activity, and the advances in technique and changes in demand relevant to particular lines of activity. It is now necessary to consider the circumstances affecting the availability of capital and its application to the processes of industry and trade.

Capital is essentially a stock. From a world-wide point of view, it is the stock of man-made equipment including goods in process; but from the point of view of Britain alone, a distinction has to be drawn between domestic capital (the equipment inside the country) and overseas capital (often called 'foreign investment'), which is a stock of claims on the products of other countries. The domestic capital contributes directly to current production of goods, while the overseas capital contributes to national income because the income derived from this capital allows the country to import more than it exports. Domestic capital is increased by construction of 'capital goods' destined for use in the country; overseas capital is increased by an excess of exports over imports. During the six decades 1880-1940 Britain was adding to her capital of both kinds, very substantially, though there was some interruption of the flows during the war period, 1914-18, and a decidedly slower accumulation of overseas capital in the inter-war period than pre-war. The capital may be owned by individuals, companies, and other private concerns (such as educational foundations), in which case it is in 'the private sector'; or it may be owned by governmental bodies (including local authorities) and is described as 'in the public sector'. This distinction applies almost entirely, in this period, to domestic capital; the additions to domestic capital were to an important and increasing extent in the public sector though additions to overseas capital were practically all private. Houses and other dwellings are reckoned as capital, and are an important part of the total; domestic equipment (furniture, kitchen goods, etc.) is somewhat anomalously excluded, expenditure thereon being reckoned as 'consumption'. Until 1920 nearly all houses were in the private sector, but since that date many of them have been in the public sector.

All additions to capital, whether domestic or overseas, private or public, have to be financed by saving, in the sense of an excess of income over current consumption; the accumulated stock of capital is the result of saving in the past. In 1880 Britain had a considerable stock of capital: in a very rough way, its value could be put at £5,000 M., comprising £4,000 M. of domestic capital (nearly half being the houses) plus £1,000 M. of overseas capital. This total, equal to somewhere around five times the national income in 1880, was the result of past accumulation. Between 1880 and 1940 the stock was increased—there was *capital accumulation*—both domestic and overseas, both public and private. In the early 1880s, when national income was not much above £1,000 M., domestic capital was growing by about £100 M. a year (of which an average of £15 M. would be in the public sector), and overseas capital was growing very irregularly, sometimes by as little as £10 M., more often by £30 M. or £40 M. in a year. At this time, that is to say, Britain was devoting 10 to 13 per cent of its output to increasing its capital equipment and claims on the outside world. All these figures are of *net* capital formation: they are additional, that is to say, to the effort that went into the replacement of equipment that was wearing out or otherwise becoming useless. (The statistical bases of such figures at this early date, it must be remembered, are exceedingly shaky, and only round figures are given here to indicate orders of magnitude.)

During the pre-1914 period, when national income was growing (£1,750 M. in 1900, £2,270 M. in 1913), the resources devoted to increasing the stock of capital at home increased relatively little. After some very lean years from 1884 to 1895, the annual increase in domestic capital rose nearly to £200 M. in the good years around 1900, but fell back again and even in the pre-war boom it was running at only £130 M. to £150 M. a year. This decline (a decline in the annual *increment* of capital, not in the existing stock) was largely a decline in house-building and in railway construction outside London; Britain was building ships faster than ever before, and was still adding greatly to the machinery of the textile and other established industries. But what did increase spectacularly in the ten years before 1914 was the overseas investment. Discouraging losses and unpaid dividends in the 1890s had kept new overseas investment at a low level until about 1905, but the figures then shot up, very soon passing £100 M. a year and probably exceeding £200 M. in the last year of peace. Thus in the last years before 1914 Britain was devoting about one-sixth of its income to increasing its capital. Much more than half of this sixth went to finance capital development in other countries, and of the remainder a large part went into new ships and equipment for the great export industries. Only about a tenth of the new capital was going into the public sector, and a twentieth into residential building. Britain was, in short, gearing itself more each year to dependence on the outside world.

The war of 1914-18 caused a serious interruption in the accumulation of capital. While there were extraordinary additions to the nation's equipment, many of these, being specially designed for the production of shells or other war material, were of little use for peacetime purposes. At the same time much of the ordinary capital stock was allowed to go unrepaired, as railway travellers at the end of the war remember too well; there was appreciable destruction, especially of ships; and there was some sale of overseas investments, to finance extraordinary imports. In such distorted conditions the quantification of net change in the nation's capital equipment is peculiarly difficult. The leading authority (Bowley) summed up his survey by remarking that: 'The world was poorer in 1919 than in 1914, though perhaps not so much poorer as reflective persons would have expected.' He reckoned that within two years after the end of the war the actual destruction was, in Britain as in some other countries, repaired, 'and the equipment as a whole was perhaps superior to that in 1914'.[1] As much could not be said of Britain's overseas capital, about one-quarter of which had been sold to pay for wartime imports.

For the years from 1924 onwards much better figures exist, thanks to the efforts of Mr. Colin Clark and others who were laying the foundations of the post-1940 official statistics of national income and capital. The amount and the nature of capital accumulation, in relation to national income, contrasted sharply with the pre-war position. Prices in general being much above pre-war, and the population having grown, the net national income was in 1924 about £4,000 M.; it rose a little above this in the later 'twenties, was rather lower through the early 'thirties, then rose perhaps to £5,000 M. by 1939. Out of this income, in 1924 only about 8 per cent was devoted to capital accumulation; in the early 'thirties the nation was doing scarcely more than maintain its capital intact, and the proportion rose no higher than 7 or at most 8 per cent in 1935-9. Of the total accumulation during the years between the wars, little represented addition to overseas capital; there was a small flow in the later 'twenties, rising to perhaps £100 M. in 1929, but British claims on overseas countries actually declined in the early 'thirties, when receipts from exports were falling far short of expenditure on imports. At home, leaving aside the very bad years 1931-3, net additions to capital were rather below £250 M. in the 1920s, and rose a little above this in the later 1930s. The composition of this domestic accumulation contrasted sharply with the pre-war emphasis on equipment of the staple industries: now, in the inter-war years, at first a third and then a half went into housing, and much of the remainder went into the construction of roads, power stations, and other public works. In the industrial field, there was some capital construction where new industries were developing. In sum, during the inter-war period most of Britain's capital accumulation took the form of housing, public works, and, on a comparatively small scale, equipment of new industries, whereas before 1914 the greater part had gone to investment in the development of the outside world and equipment of her great export industries. It would be wrong to conclude that the change implied either more or less wasteful use of the nation's resources. In the first two decades of the century, the 1½ million houses built had not gone far towards replacing old houses and providing for the 6 millions' increase in

[1] A. L. Bowley, *Some Economic Consequences of the Great War* (London, 1930), p. 91.

population. In these circumstances, it was not obviously extravagant to devote 2 or 3 per cent of national income to new houses that would be used for decades, any more than it was extravagant before 1914 to devote 5 to 10 per cent of national income to overseas investment. In any case, no one made the decision on this national scale; these national aggregates resulted from countless individual decisions, unplanned by governments and co-ordinated only by the imperfect working of the markets.

The individual decisions were of three kinds: decisions to spend less than current income (the decision to 'save'); decisions to use the savings for buying securities (domestic or overseas) or for placing with banks, insurance companies, or other financial institutions; and decisions to spend on the construction of capital goods (including houses). To a considerable extent, the decisions to save and the decisions to spend on capital construction are made by different people, and it is a function of the country's financial institutions (banks and financial businesses of great variety) to put the savings at the disposal of the capital-spenders. Changes in this financial mechanism—'the capital market', in a broad sense—are therefore outlined below, as among the factors affecting the efficiency of the economic system. The decisions to save are taken by individuals, but also to an important extent by joint-stock companies which are responsible for much of the nation's industrial organization and for most of the decisions to spend on capital goods for direct industrial use. During the decades 1880-1940 there was a rapid spread of this form of organization, and this may conveniently be summarized at this point, before the development of the capital market itself is reviewed.

Joint-stock companies began to grow rapidly in number after the limited liability legislation of the late 1850s, consolidated in an Act of 1862. Amending legislation in 1900 and 1908 made life rather more difficult for fraudulent promoters and directors of companies, and in 1929 these steps were carried much further. By legislation in 1907-8 'private companies', restricted to fifty shareholders, were allowed to limit the liabilities of their shareholders. As the price of freedom from publication of balance-sheets, etc., they were precluded from inviting the public to subscribe capital. The private companies registered under these provisions remained mainly family businesses but they were able to draw capital from somewhat wider circles and, unlike private partnerships, they were not subject to legal upheaval when any shareholder died.

Among the early registrations of public joint-stock companies an appreciable proportion—probably a third—were for one reason or another abortive, and of the remainder ('effective' registrations) about a quarter were defunct within five years, generally through fraud, ignorance, or gross mismanagement. Allowing for these casualties, there were probably between 8,000 and 10,000 limited joint-stock companies in existence at the beginning of 1880, and new foundations were coming thick and fast. In the next four years (1880-3) there were over 2,500 new public companies and 800 private. Among the public companies, the largest groups were 'Mines and Lands' (124 colonial and 184 foreign) besides 166 coal-, iron-, or lead-mining companies at home. Shipping accounted for 383 public and 131 private companies, many of them being owners of single ships. Eighty public companies and 9 private companies foretold, by their classification 'Electrical', a new age; there had been none of them at all until 1878. Hotels and restaurants accounted for nearly 200, most of them public companies; the food and provisions group was about as large, though fewer of these were public. 'Land and building' accounted for 152 in all, but there were also 84 for bricks, tiles, and cement. Ironworks, engineering, and shipbuilding totalled 254. Financial undertakings were 143, but 51 of these were 'Petty Lending'.

By 1913 (six years after the law had recognized private companies) the company habit had spread far into mining and manufacturing, and was gaining more slowly among the hundreds of thousands of wholesalers and retailers. At that date some 60,000 companies were operating in the U.K., with a paid-up capital of about £2,500 M. New registrations were coming along at 6,000 or 7,000 a year. About 2,000 a year were dropping out; not necessarily dropping out of business, for many were voluntarily liquidated on being amalgamated with others. The number of public companies actually reached its all-time maximum, just below 15,000, in 1936; but private companies continued to increase and reached 150,000 at the outbreak of war. The paid-up capital of public companies was then, at £4,130 M., just over twice that of the private companies; the average was twenty times as much for a public as for a private company. What was happening was broadly that the big companies were getting bigger but not more numerous, and that the steady drift of family businesses into the private-company form was still continuing. For an entirely new business to start as a company remained rare; almost invariably a company began life by taking over some existing business. This would sometimes be the prelude to an abrupt increase of scale or scope, but many private companies remained very small, as is evidenced by the average capital of less than £13,000. At the other extreme were the giant public companies; these were indeed 'companies', for their millions of pounds of capital would be spread over thousands of shareholders, the individual holdings averaging as little as £200 or £300.

The advantage of the new form of business organization was that it facilitated the collection, from a large number of individuals who need have no other connexion with the firm, of amounts of capital that were individually small but added up to the huge sums necessary for exploitation of the technical possibilities of large-scale production. The company form therefore tended to appear earlier in industries where these technical possibilities were most obvious. (In an extreme case, the railways, special legal powers had anticipated the general company legislation.) Development was by fits and starts, almost a matter of fashion in each particular industrial group. Breweries, for example, were becoming companies thick and fast in the late 'eighties (Guinness 'went company' in 1886); cotton spinning in Lancashire had the fashion, in a restricted way, in the 1900s, and less discriminatingly in 1919-20. In some of the older industries, however, where thrifty habits had persisted in great industrial families, the change-over was delayed; iron and steel was such a case, some of the largest firms remaining family partnerships well into the twentieth century. As taxation on inheritances rose, the process of conversion of partnerships into companies was accelerated, even where developments in the techniques of production were not forcing enlargement of the business units. Once the change was made, a firm could grow more easily; and firms did grow, so that by 1935 55 per cent of the country's labour force was employed in business units with 500 or more employees each.

The ability of the individual firm to grow, once it had become a public company, was strikingly demonstrated in the thirty years 1890-1920, when a few firms, whose names became household words, achieved dominating positions in their industries. Such were the Distillers Company in whisky, Lever Brothers in soap, Bryant & May in matches, J. & P. Coats in sewing cotton, the United Alkali Company and Brunner Mond in heavy chemicals, Nobel Industries in explosives, and the Imperial Tobacco Company. Such economic theory as was grasped by thinking Englishmen still centred round the virtues of perfect competition, and the concentration of an industry into a single firm was considered a major threat to economical use of resources. The dangers were not confined to concentration of production in single firms, for there were many other industries in which firms covering most or all of the output were associated in monopolistic regulation of markets. The drift towards monopolistic combinations—'trusts' as, following American usage, they were increasingly labelled—became a minor worry of government when, in 1916-18, the problems of industrial reconstruction were surveyed, and a Committee on Trusts was appointed in 1918 to consider what action should be taken to safeguard the public interest. The Committee recommended nothing more drastic than collection of information, and a succession of official reports on individual industries followed. In the event, the drift was allowed to continue, and 1927 saw the biggest industrial combination of all when Imperial Chemical Industries was formed by the merging of four firms that were already giants in their own right.

The company fashion, especially the growth of the large public companies, was characteristic of mining and manufacture; it scarcely touched agriculture. The large-scale public utilities, such as railways, canals, and waterworks, had been joint-stock companies from the start, and it was the technical advantage of increasing the scale of production that made adoption of the company form so popular in mining and manufacture during this period. There remained important sectors of economic activity where the family firm or private partnership remained normal or gave way to public joint-stock companies only in special cases. Most notable of these sectors were retail trade and the 'service' or 'craft' businesses closely associated with retail trade. The basic reason is simple enough. A thousand motor-cars, or a thousand ordinary-sized shirts, can most economically be made by simple repetition of certain processes, and the most economical organization of production is in large agglomerations of capital and workpeople. But while there may be one sensible way of making a car or a radio set, there are a thousand ways in which it can go wrong and need local attention by a servicing agent. There are a thousand ways in which people may be persuaded to buy cars, or radio sets. And when it comes to a service like hairdressing, every head requires individual attention. So, although the manufacture of novel articles for the consumer was rapidly concentrated in large industrial units, the rise of these new industries brought in its train swarms of small retail outlets. For these and other reasons, independent shops remained exceedingly numerous, despite the spectacular growth of some large organizations. How many shops there were in the late nineteenth century is unknown; for the 1930s there is good authority for 600,000 as the order of magnitude.

In number, the great majority of the 600,000 were little shops, owned by individuals or partnerships relying on their own capital supplemented by easy credit from wholesalers and, sometimes, from banks. For most of these, the annual turnover was probably less than £3,000. At the other end of the scale, in the inter-war period, were the thousand department stores, among which about a dozen had each a turnover exceeding a million pounds a year. The multiple shops, though individually often quite small, were owned and run by large joint-stock companies; twelve firms each had more than 500 branches. The department stores and multiple shops together were in the 'thirties doing about a quarter of the country's retail trade, as compared with less than 10 per cent in 1910. The co-operative societies (a class by itself, including many small but also some very large organizations) were also growing: $7\frac{1}{2}$ per cent of the total trade in 1910, 10 per cent in the 1930s.

These larger organizations in retail trade had all made an appearance before 1880, but most of their development belongs to the decades since that date. The co-operative movement had, it is true, put down strong roots in the north country in the middle decades of the nineteenth century; particularly it had attracted a large proportion of the trade in the smaller industrial and mining towns. By 1900 every place of any size had its 'co-op'; thereafter the increase was by the opening of branch shops and increase in membership (to $8\frac{1}{2}$ millions in 1939). Total sales quadrupled between 1880 and 1910, and the 1910 figure was (after allowing for price inflation) doubled again by 1939. Typically the co-operatives were selling, by austerely simple methods, foodstuffs and the cheaper clothing but, especially as they spread southward, they widened their range and became much more like other shops catering for the broad run of working-class shoppers. They continued to rely for their capital on the savings of members, largely in the form of undrawn dividends on purchases; they had accumulated £200 M. before 1939.

The co-operatives and the multiple shops gained ground rapidly in the decades before 1914 partly because their insistence on cash payment enabled them to undercut rivals who had to allow a wide margin for bad debts and the cost of credit. The advantage was such that some of the multiples—at least two of the chemists' chains among them—put the word 'Cash' in their names. Along with this popularization of cash payments went a reduction of adulteration and similar practices which had been particularly rife in the grocery trades. Once competition began to push in this direction—and the rise of the co-operative societies was an important influence of this kind—the buying public sharpened its awareness and supported new legal restrictions and effective administration (e.g. of Weights and Measures Acts) by the new local government authorities. All such changes had connexion also with the branding of consumption goods and the development of advertising. Resale price maintenance—the fixing of the retail price by the manufacturing supplier—was spreading after 1890, and helped to change the habits of shoppers and shopkeepers. In 1886 Levers, the soap firm, spent only £50 on advertising, but that was the year when Millais's painting 'Bubbles' was bought by Pears to incite people to buy soap, and in the next twenty years Levers spent £2 M. on advertising. 'Bovril' became another typical item on the shopping-list: originally a meat extract used in French fortresses in the war of 1870, it was caught up in England's war on drunkenness and in the twentieth century it won nation-wide popularity by a poster campaign that made advertising history.

The development of advertisement in national newspapers and posters probably helped to maintain the large number of little shops alongside the multiples, the co-operatives, and the department stores, which were absorbing much of the increased business as the total national income increased. It was easy enough for the little shop to stock the goods that were made known by the manufacturers' advertisements, and resale price maintenance precluded the large store from undercutting the little man. Later in the period, multiple stores of the miscellaneous type (Woolworths and Marks and Spencers) began to overcome this by using brand names of their own, as the 'cash chemists' had done from the beginning. In these later years the larger units were also gaining from the greater ease, as country buses multiplied, of getting into town on a shopping expedition. The big shops did not, however, have things all their own way, for the housewife cannot always go off on a major shopping expedition, and as the new housing estates sprawled over the country-side there was plenty of opportunity for new little shops with the advantage of being 'just round the corner'. Some of the changes in the pattern of consumption were working the same way: the English people were buying more fruit and vegetables, and the proliferation of little greengrocers was a feature of the inter-war decades.

The capital for little shops continued to come, as for generations past, from a miscellany of unorganized sources: family savings (especially profits ploughed back in successful businesses), trade credit from wholesale and manufacturing suppliers, mortgages, and banks. Even for the biggest retail units the sources of capital were not much different until the very end of the period. London department stores were 'going company' late in the nineteenth century, but for many years they remained essentially family concerns, and when they did become public companies there was little trading in their shares and public issues were rare.

In this independence of the Stock Exchange and other parts of the 'London capital market' retail trade was like most other industries and trades. Overwhelmingly the Stock Exchange until 1914 was dealing in the debts of governments—British, Dominion, Colonial, and Foreign—and in the capital of the world's railways. The total of securities quoted on the Stock Exchange was £3,641 M. in 1883, and governments and railways accounted for £3,372 M. of these. By 1933 the total had grown to £18,476 M., and governments and railways still accounted for 80 per cent; commercial and industrial securities had become quite prominent in daily press reports, but were still only about one-tenth of the total of securities in existence. The New York stock market's speculative fever in the late 1920s had been world-wide news and had made the public much more aware of the increasing variety of marketable securities, as was shown by London's own speculative outbreak in 1927-8. This bubble—exploited mainly by promoters in some of the new industries—burst so quickly that it served mainly to prompt an overdue revision of the Companies Acts, and rather confirmed the high-standing new-issue houses in their neglect of home industry. The ways of these firms in marketing newly created stocks and shares changed very little during the whole period, the only notable development being the rise, in the late decades of the nineteenth century, of the practice of 'underwriting' new issues. An underwriter guarantees to buy any of the offered new securities not subscribed for by the public; the adoption of this practice made it safe for issuers to fix the prices when they published the prospectus. A fixed price is always more attractive for the raiser of capital, and issues 'by tender' therefore fell out of common practice as underwriting came in.

The development of underwriting of new issues was a symptom of the rapid growth during these decades of a great array of specialized financial institutions in the City of London. This had two facets: the growth of

London's activity as the financial centre of the world, and the growth of London as the home, and not just the correspondent, of financial institutions concerned with finding employment for a great part of individual savings.

As the leading international financial centre—a place where payments arising in business across frontiers were arranged, and foreign traders borrowed and lent money freely—London was already well established by the middle of the nineteenth century. Its activity of this kind greatly increased between 1880 and 1914. The firms most fully concerned in international business were the merchant bankers, or 'Accepting Houses' as they were increasingly called;[1] they continued to occupy themselves almost exclusively with international business, both temporary finance and the issue of long-term securities. The market in bills of exchange, after a bad shaking in the Overend Gurney crisis in 1866, experienced a tremendous expansion of its international business until 1914; it almost completely shed its business in the finance of internal trade. In bringing to the London market this great flow of bills of exchange, the traditional merchant banks were now supplemented by the great overseas banks, many of which had been founded with British capital and London head offices in the 1860s. All this side of London's business was seriously curtailed, though never completely stopped, by the 1914-18 war. After the war it revived, for a time, but in the depression of international trade in the 1930s it shrank to pitiful proportions.

From the great nineteenth-century development of international business the ordinary English and Scottish 'domestic' banks stood almost entirely aside. They reckoned to take deposits from residents (including companies) and to employ their funds mainly in short-term lending to internal business. A small part went into government securities; another small part went into bills of exchange, and so helped to finance international business but this, conducted only through the London money market, did not involve the banks in direct international contacts. In the 'eighties there were still in England and Wales about 240 private banks (small partnerships) with few branches, alongside 120 joint-stock banks of varying size. Only about a dozen of these joint-stock banks had more than fifty branches each. The scene was, however,

---

[1] The term 'Accepting House' is derived from the business of 'accepting' bills of exchange; by accepting a bill, a merchant banker (or anyone else) accepted the obligation to pay the bill at its due date.

already being changed by a trickle of amalgamations, especially by private banks' and little joint-stock banks' selling out to the larger joint-stock banks. The trickle became a stream after 1890, and the formation of Barclays Bank out of the great Quaker connexion of private banks was a sign of the times. By 1913 the number of joint-stock banks was down to forty (though these had 6,000 branches) and about a dozen private banks clung to their independence. Then during the war the leading banks entered on a final race for bigness, and the 'Big Five' emerged each with a branch network covering most of England and between them doing five-sixths of the domestic banking business. Scotland, where joint-stock banks with numerous branches had been earlier established, was in appearance little affected by the amalgamation movement, the ten banks with 1,000 branches (in total) becoming eight with 1,800 branches. Below the surface there was more change, for some of these Scottish banks were bought by the English giants. In the inter-war years one of the remaining independent Scottish banks (the Royal Bank of Scotland) invaded England by absorbing two of the small English banks, but this oddity did not seriously modify the dominance of the scene by the five giants with their head offices in London and branches on the main street-corners up and down the country.

The business habits of the banks altered surprisingly little while this structural revolution was going on, or indeed after its completion. Very cautiously they began to undertake for their customers more foreign business, and in the 1920s this had become usual, though the foreign departments generally confined themselves to operation through correspondent banks, not offices of their own beyond the sea. They still reckoned to do most of their lending on a temporary basis for internal business, and found especially numerous outlets in lending to farmers, builders, and shopkeepers of every size. In the kind of business they would finance, the bankers were never as rigid as their textbooks suggested; but there were grumblings that the absorption of little country banks by the London giants meant more working by rule and less attention to the peculiar needs of small business. As a general charge this was certainly unjust, but perhaps in the first decades of their bigness some of the giants did over-centralize and become less flexible in meeting their customers' needs. Whether or not this rigidity on the lending side was enough to affect seriously the flow of capital into useful channels, it is certain that the conservatism of the banks on the deposit side did

F

limit their growth and the part they were able to play in the application of the nation's capital. For they stood aside almost completely from the spread of thrift in the working and lower middle classes. Between 1880 and 1913, deposits in the Post Office and Trustee Savings Banks rose from £80 M. to £256 M.; their growth then slowed as competing channels such as National Savings Certificates appeared, but even in the difficult 'thirties deposits almost doubled, to reach £800 M. in 1939. Most significantly, the joint-stock banks stood aside from the movement to home-ownership, leaving to the building societies work for which their own branch systems were well suited. There were already some 1,500 of these building societies established before 1880, with purely local memberships (totalling perhaps half a million) and business. By 1908 there were 1,800 building societies, with £73 M. mainly in mortgage loans on owner-occupied houses. Then began a slow process of amalgamation especially by the rise of multi-branch societies based on some of the strongest societies in the north of England. Once private building got going in the 'twenties the building societies went ahead by leaps and bounds. Between 1922 and 1939, while the number of societies went down from 1,200 to 960, their balance-sheet totals rose more than sevenfold: during the 'thirties they were collecting and lending £50 M. a year, from 3 million investors and to 1·5 million borrowers.

Regular 'contractual' saving, as by monthly contribution to a building society, was in the later decades becoming almost the typical way of saving. Another channel for these contractual savings was in life assurance. In earlier decades there had been some accumulation in these companies, but most of the premiums had been absorbed in current claims. In the 1930s, however, the spread of pension schemes gave the business fresh impetus and premiums rose well above claims, so that the total funds in the business were rising by about £70 M. a year. A few of the assurance companies were becoming more venturesome in their investments: the proportion of life funds invested in ordinary shares crept up to 9 per cent by 1937. The weight of new saving going through 'institutional' channels, especially the savings banks and assurance companies, into the market for government securities would have had awkward effects had the National Debt remained on its 1913 scale; but the tenfold increase of the Debt by the 1914-18 war made the supply of these securities superabundant, enough indeed to scare people into talk of a Capital Levy to reduce the Debt. The talk died down, and the nation accommodated itself to the swollen Debt. In the 1930s the Debt in a broad sense was actually increasing, for local government and other public authorities borrowed large sums, but this increase in public debt was merely matching a relative increase in governmental activity. There was in fact some switch of national economic activity—involving the employment of capital—from the private sector to the public sector. The radio broadcasting service was a governmental activity almost from the start, and electricity generation was substantially nationalized in 1926, just before its big development. (More radical ideas for government or workers' control of industry had been aired before 1920, but the 1920s and 1930s settled for the 'public board' method of public ownership.) Most of the developments in financial institutions meant a growing appetite for 'safe' investment of institutional savings, so that there was no difficulty in absorbing the capital liabilities of the growing public sector. Supporting the private sector, on the other hand, was a new variety of investment trust: the 'unit trusts' appearing in the 1930s opened the way for much more widespread interest of small savers in ordinary shares. Like other developments popularizing ordinary shareholding, however, these new channels facilitated the attraction of capital into the established industrial giants, not the little firms, some of which could have put much more capital to use in new industrial developments that were badly needed to replace the decayed export industries of pre-1914 Britain.

At the centre of the structure of financial institutions stood the Bank of England. It remained in private ownership until 1946, but the exclusively public nature of its responsibilities was more or less accepted throughout the period and was explicitly acknowledged by its Governor in the inter-war years. Its leadership in the City of London was strengthened at the time of the Baring crisis in 1890 and became even more decided when, after 1920, it re-elected Montagu Norman as Governor year after year, instead of having a new hand at the helm every second year. Until 1914 it was primarily engaged in an almost automatic maintenance of the gold value of sterling by using Bank Rate to influence international capital movements. Its success in that period, in the propitious circumstance of Britain's long export boom, led to undue confidence in its power. After the war Britain's international trading position was (as has been seen in Chapter 2) altogether weaker, but the implications of this for the Bank were underrated when Britain returned to a fixed exchange rate policy (the gold standard) in 1925. The actions of the Bank in the ensuing years probably had little effect either good or ill, but its identification with a policy that seemed in retrospect to have sacrificed British industrial interests to the international interests of the financial institutions helped to stoke the fires of criticism. When in 1929, for the first time in seventy years, a major official inquiry, the Macmillan Committee, was mounted, the terms of reference were significant: 'To inquire into banking, finance and credit, paying regard to the factors both internal and international which govern their operation, and to make recommendations calculated to enable these agencies to promote the development of trade and commerce and the employment of labour.' It so happened that at this very moment world trade was just beginning its spin down into the most severe depression known to living memory, and the few critical comments and constructive proposals the Macmillan Committee made on the financial system's work as a mobilizer of capital were lost in the nation's helplessness in the face of a situation that was beyond any tinkering with institutions or minor turns in economic policy.

In the new climate of opinion of which the Macmillan Report was symptomatic, the reaction of the Bank of England to the onset of world depression was more helpful than in the slump of 1921-2. Yet on this occasion once again depression was aggravated by traditional balanced-budget policies in Britain as in other countries, and in such conditions monetary ease and (from 1931) a flexible exchange rate were of little avail. The illusion of a glut of capital was created simply because almost everyone was scared off useful investment, and what saving survived was largely absorbed in the finance of other people's losses. When revival did come, its kernel was an increase in house-building, and for the finance of this activity and the related public works the building societies and local government authorities were the major channels. The depressed areas of the old export industries remained hopelessly under-employed. The government did hesitantly recognize that positive action would have to be taken to help them, and special facilities were created for the establishment of new industrial works. For the label 'Depressed Areas' the supposedly less depressing term 'Special Areas' was substituted, but nothing radical was done to stimulate the flow of capital and business enterprise that was needed to absorb the surplus labour in the old industrial areas. Nor, despite the continuance of very low interest rates, did the financial institutions of Britain seem able to channel capital into developments that would absorb the labour into other areas. The best that could be said was that, unlike the financial institutions of many other countries, those of London had not by their own collapse aggravated the depression; but they were powerless either to stimulate total demand or to promote the radical redistribution of national resources that was required.

10

The Unanswered Questions

A S W A S R E M A R K E D in the opening chapter of this book, economic history is concerned with man's varying success in mastering 'the economic problem' of securing an increase in his material welfare. The economic historian seeks the facts on the flow of goods and services constituting income and, studying the chronological sequence, he theorizes—and speculates—on the causes of change. It is in this sense that this book is a sketch of—and not a treatise on—the economic history of England from 1880 until the outbreak of war in 1939. After nine chapters, many questions remain unanswered; it would therefore be unfitting for this final chapter to attempt a summary of conclusions. Instead, it may be useful—especially for readers who wish to probe further into the subject—to indicate some of the questions to which the previous chapters provide no answers.

The unanswered questions are of four kinds. First, many aspects of English economic life in this period have been ignored, or scarcely touched upon, because room could not be found in such a little book, although the main facts may be well established and their relevance to the course of change well understood by authors whose work might have been drawn upon. Secondly, there are questions that remain unanswered because the facts are not known, although the nature of these facts is such that historians can expect them to emerge in course of time. Thirdly, there are problems yet unsolved because, though many relevant facts are already known, there has been insufficient analysis of these facts. The unanswered questions in all these three groups are bound to be exceedingly numerous for a period so close to today; a plethora of detail is known, yet there has been no time to uncover some of the most interesting facts, and little opportunity for analysis detached from the prejudice and passion of those who lived through the events. The fourth group is quite different: it is of the questions that never can be answered with any assurance, because the relevant facts can never be known, so that analysis must be blurred by judgement and opinions will differ to the end of the world.

Some idea of the economic activities not discussed in earlier chapters may be gained from the occupational summaries of the 1881 Census. There were four groups each with over a million people occupied: domestic service, 1,804,000; agriculture, 1,279,000; mining (mostly coal), 1,278,000; and textiles, 1,054,000. Five other groups each included between half a million and a million: dressmaking and tailoring, 981,000; work on houses, furniture, and decoration, 787,000; general mechanics and labourers (a miscellany, not a true 'occupational group'), 695,000; transport, 663,000; and food and lodging, 629,000. Of these eight groups (omitting the general labourers), little has been said here of any except those in agriculture, coal-mining, and cotton textiles. The reader must not suppose that the other 5 or 6 million workers were in occupations that underwent no change during this period. There was, however, little change in either the techniques or the organization of most of them. Domestic service, for example, meant almost throughout the period household chores without any aid from electric cleaners, though the arduousness of carpet-sweeping was eased by vacuum cleaners first patented in 1901. The hundreds of thousands of servants were spread over a vast number of places of employment. In the late nineteenth century, people with £500 a year would employ a cook and a maid. 'To employ anything masculine, however diminutive', said Mrs. Beeton, 'was the first sign of affluence', and it was only in the 'great houses' of town and country that young, middle-aged, and elderly servants of both sexes could avoid loneliness, at the expense of orderly regimentation under the butler (at £50 or £60 a year 'all found') and the housekeeper (at £50). The 1914 war caused a great upheaval in all this: the great houses dwindled rapidly, and the relative rise of women's wages combined with other forces to break middle-class standards of domestic employment.

The upset of the labour market by the 1914 war probably had more lasting effects on women's employment in the south and east than in the 'Industrial Revolution areas' of the north where women had for generations worked 'in the mill' in the textile areas or where—as in the coalfields—women continued after as before the war to have virtually no opportunities. The proportion of occupied to unoccupied females (all ages) was never far from 1 to 2; it was falling slowly between 1881 and 1914, then almost reverted to the 1881 level until 1931. In the south-eastern half of the country the scope for women was gradually widened as the new industries developed, and especially in the London area type-writing and other office employment steadily increased, and this balanced the decline in domestic service and agriculture. In textiles, employment of women was always important and the kind of work they had to do changed hardly at all. There was some difference of experience between cotton in Lancashire (discussed in Chapter 6) and the woollen and worsted industry of the West Riding. There was between 1880 and 1940 a considerable increase in productivity in the West Riding industry, and, as in cotton on the other side of the Pennines, this resulted from improvement, but not technical revolution, in the machinery. Like the cotton industry, the woollen industry flourished in the pre-war genera-tion, but it was home demand rather than export demand here that was responsible for the pre-1914 boom, and, contrasting even more sharply with cotton, it was a failure of home demand that was responsible for dull days in the inter-war period. (The major factor was probably the change in fashion, encouraged by the appearance of new materials.) In terms of employment the upshot was that the total hardly moved beyond the range 230,000-270,000 (of both sexes). In numbers occupied, the business of making up the various textile fabrics into clothes was in 1881 almost as big as all the textile industries put together. These dress-making and tailoring trades were very widely spread, in tiny units, all over the country, though there were big concentrations of them in the East End of London. In the inter-war years factory-made clothes began to gain at the cheaper end of the trade; particularly, new chains of shops were linked with modern clothing factories in Yorkshire and elsewhere, while the one-man bespoke tailoring business and the local dressmaker entered their long decline.

There were other industries where the small business, employing a few craftsmen and unskilled labourers, was more retentive than in the clothing trades. A large proportion of the 787,000 recorded in the 1881 Census as 'working and dealing in houses, furniture, and decoration' were in the building trades, and these continued throughout the period to follow the centuries-old craft techniques, and to be organized mostly in small firms. In the furniture trades there was probably more change, both in the actual manufacture and in the channels of trade. Just what was the structure of such industries as these seems likely to remain one of the unanswered questions, for the basic information was not collected in any detail, though much can be learned from surviving scraps of the kind that is the economic historian's only material when studying times before Giffen's 'statistical century'. One would also like to know more than is ever likely to emerge about the price-fixing methods of these various trades, for it is probable that changes in price-fixing methods, consequent upon the transition from the one-man firm to the industrial colossus, have had important implications for the working of the economic system.

One major group of occupations scarcely mentioned in earlier chapters is the transport group. Most of the 663,000 employees in 1881 were on the railways, already large undertakings foreshadowing the problems of organization and price-fixing that were to spread to a much wider field in the twentieth century. In the first decades the railways met the competition only of horse and cart and, on some routes, coastal shipping; but the great days of railway expansion were over, and the only new main line, the Great Central (1899), never paid its way. The loss fell on shareholders, for the railways were still privately owned. Gladstone's nationalization threat had never seemed real, and the centralized government control in the 1914-18 war was quickly followed by return to private hands. Almost immediately, however, the railways were compulsorily merged into four gigantic groups, and it was these groups which in the 'thirties began to suffer substantially from the new road competition. When this competition put an altogether new complexion on railway pricing problems, there could no longer be any pretence that the old-fashioned economics of private enterprise provided all the answers.

In the forty years before 1920 the ruling ideas of the virtues of private enterprise had been increasingly challenged, and socialistic reformers had propounded general schemes of public ownership and control not only for the railways but also for a wide range of other businesses. The nineteenth-century Fabian socialists thought in terms of government departments and direct political control; then between 1900 and 1920 ideas of workers' control ('syndicalism') gained ground. By the time public opinion was accepting the inevitability of some new form of economic organization for special types of activity (railways, broadcasting, electricity supply, etc.), the idea had arisen that control of such undertakings should be vested neither in government departments nor in workers' organizations but in 'Public Boards' standing aside from the political scene yet nevertheless representing a balance of interests of consumers, workers, and government. The idea was ventilated notably in the Liberal Party's 'Yellow Book' at the end of the 1920s. These 'Public Boards' then became common as the managers of large undertakings of the public utility type; an example was the London Passenger Transport Board, established in 1933 with a monopoly of underground railways, trams, and buses. The boards of the newly nationalized industries after 1945 closely followed this pattern of development.

There were other ways in which more of the country's resources were passing out of the control of private enterprise. There has been mention in earlier chapters of elements in the growth of the *public sector*. Housing, social security, education, municipal trading in electricity and transport, a public telephone system: all these and other developments meant an increasing role for government in the ordinary economic life of the country. The relative importance of the public sector can be measured by showing the total payments by all governmental bodies as a percentage of national income: it was not much above 10 per cent before 1900, rose to around 15 in 1900-14, and then (after its wartime aberration) was 30 or a little higher in the 1920s and 1930s.[1] In the 'eighties, when 125,000 people were in the Armed Forces, defence accounted for one-fortieth of the national income; international tensions forced this upward long before 1914 but it was allowed to drop back, almost to one-fortieth again, in the economy campaigns just before fears of Hitler and Mussolini pushed it up in 1935-9. About equally important in the pre-1914 expansion of the public sector were the social security measures of the Asquith Government (1908-15) and the growth of municipal trading in electricity, gas, and other services. This last was self-financing, but much of the new social expenditure and all the defence expenditure fell on taxation, and the coincidence of their growth before 1914 forced a major revision of the tax system.

Actually it was expenditure on the troubled frontiers of Empire in the 'eighties that put an end to Gladstone's pipe-dream of abolition of the income-tax and set the nation on its path of increasing reliance on direct taxation of income and capital. The proportion of these 'direct' taxes in the total doubled between 1880 and 1900, and was almost to

[1] Some government payments (e.g. social insurance benefits) are purely 'transfers', in that the government is not purchasing goods and services. If all transfer payments were excluded, the three percentages would be more like 9, 13, and 24.

double again before the Second World War. A generation that believed that wealth was best left 'to fructify in the pockets of the people' found death duties less repugnant than steeper taxation of income, and reform of the death duties, planned by Lord Randolph Churchill in the 'eighties and implemented by Harcourt in 1894, was the prelude to their progressive increase. At this time income-tax was only 8d. in the pound, and the duties on drink and tobacco brought in half the total revenue. After 1900, however, income-tax never went below 11d. (1903-4), and this and the reformed death duties were already taking an increasing share of the burden before the new Liberal Government (1906) brought radical ideas of contribution by the wealthy. Income-tax went up to 1s. 2d. and was supplemented by a new super-tax of 6d. in the pound on incomes over £5,000, and by two steps the death duties were stiffened; the 'graduation' of the tax system as a whole was transformed. In the 1914-18 war the process was carried much further, the standard rate of income-tax going to 6s. and super-tax to another 6s. After that, there was no going back, either in total burdens or in the distribution of taxation: in the middle 1920s the commodity taxes were providing only one-third of the total, although they now included taxes on motoring. In the 'economy' days of the early 1930s, when defence expenditure was skimped and low interest rates meant a cheap National Debt, income-tax was brought down to 4s. 6d. (with super-tax rates ranging up to 8s. 3d.), but rearmament, besides occasioning the innovation of a National Defence Contribution in 1937, forced the income-tax to 5s. 6d. in the last peacetime budget.

Although in the final phase it was defence expenditure that pushed taxation—indirect as well as direct—up to new peacetime heights, in comparison with 1913 the rise in the cost of government had been due more to the social services and the cost of the National Debt. Under both these headings the big change was already fully felt by 1930, when social services were costing around £500 M. as compared with £120 M. in 1913 and £22 M. in 1890. As a proportion of national income, the cost of the embryo Welfare State actually declined in the 'thirties; after that, the social problems of the Second World War did even more than the recruiting problems of the First World War to make the nation feel that it had been extravagantly niggardly.

Besides spending the proceeds of taxation, and in wartime also very large borrowed funds, the central and other governmental bodies have channelled real resources through their hands by appreciable borrowing for works of a capital nature. Though growing steadily—especially for development of tramways, electricity, and other municipal services—before 1914, the sums had been relatively small, totalling perhaps £20 M. in 1913. Between the wars it was on a much higher scale; the peak of £120 M. in 1927-8 represented, say, three or four times as much work as the pre-war £20 M. Housing was taking a large part of the increase. There was also extension of electricity stations; the new Central Electricity Generating Board (1926) was at work on the national grid, but local authorities were still responsible for much of the local capital construction. Roads were being built on a new scale, though most of this expenditure was covered by taxation in one way or another.

Altogether, taking central and local authorities, and capital as well as current expenditure, public expenditure represented nearly one-third of national income in the 1930s, three times as high a proportion as fifty years earlier. This did not mean that the nation consisted one-third of bureaucrats: of the £1,400 M. or so paid out by public bodies much went in the form of 'transfers' (pensions, interest to bondholders, etc.) and another big slice in purchase of goods. Those in direct government employment increased from 350,000 or 400,000 in 1881 to 1,800,000 in 1931; but in this total are included most schoolteachers, all policemen and post office workers, many gas, electricity, and water employees, and all the soldiers, sailors, and airmen. The civil servants, in the ordinary sense of those engaged by the central government in general administration, had their wartime expansion slashed by a hostile public opinion after 1919, and numbered no more than 50,000 in 1931. In no sense was the British economy run from Whitehall; but it was becoming a 'Mixed Economy' in which a growing public sector (including semi-autonomous boards which were large employers of labour) existed alongside a private sector which included a multitude of tiny firms as well as the gigantic enterprises.

This was not the kind of economic system about which the great economic treatises of the nineteenth century had been written, and it is not surprising that there remain many puzzles about the way it functioned. The broad behaviour of prices has often been discussed but without convincing result. In the nineteenth century—possibly as a result of the Industrial and Agricultural Revolutions and the extension of overseas trade—prices of commodities perhaps became more subject to prolonged swings up and down. There was such a swing downward in the general level of prices from about 1873 until about 1896, followed by an upward swing lasting through to 1914. At first sight it is tempting to associate these swings with changes in the supply of gold, operating through changes in the supply of money which was based on gold; but on further examination such a theory raises more questions than it answers. It is perhaps more profitable to approach this problem by looking at the individual prices whose behaviour dominated the movement of 'the general level of prices'. Following this course, the outstanding fact is that the fall in prices in 1873-96 was essentially a crash in the prices of imported food and raw materials: between 1880 and 1895 the level of import prices fell by 31 per cent, and an even more violent crash in import prices, by 36 per cent in 1929-33, dominated the behaviour of 'the general level of prices' in the inter-war period.

On the side of costs of production, there is little in the behaviour of British wage-rates to explain movements in general prices, except in the upheaval of 1914-22, when prices swung upward under the impress of extraordinary government spending and then down with an all-round cutting of wage-rates in the phase of post-war adjustment. Earlier —as again after 1922—wage-rates had been decidedly sticky, and were probably becoming increasingly so: the wage-reductions in the bad years were trivial in the 'eighties and in 1907-8, and hardly noticeable in the 'nineties. With this stickiness of wages went a stability of the prices of manufactured goods—and accordingly of many British exports— relatively to the more fluid prices of imports. When the latter tumbled, each pound's worth of British exports meant a substantially unchanged working-time of British labour but each pound paid for a much larger amount of food and raw materials than before. It was this favourable movement of 'the terms of trade' with the outside world that was the main element in the rise in real national income per head in the two phases when it was rising most rapidly. If the causes of this fall in import prices—and so of the rise in real income—are sought, the answer is not that there was any greater effort, or greater technical skill or greater effectiveness, of labour in this country during the years when income was rising most rapidly. In the earlier of the two phases (mid-'seventies to mid-'nineties) the British contribution to the cheapening of food and raw materials was rather to be found in the inventiveness of an earlier generation, now fructifying in the cheapening of transport from the new cornlands of the world, in the investment funds that had been pouring through London to the outside world, and in the earlier enterprise of Scots and Englishmen who went to join the agricultural potentialities of distant lands with the investment funds provided by the people who stayed at home. All these and many other strands enter into the texture that we bluntly summarize in the words 'economic growth'.

It seems likely that the slowing down, in the rise in real income, for twenty years after the mid-'nineties was due to the exhaustion of this particular coincidence of favourable factors rather than to any deep-seated failure of the technical abilities of British labour or of the enterprise of British employers. When in the 1920s Englishmen strove for a living in a world disorganized after four years of war, they saw their export trades apparently defeated by monetary instability which seemed to strangle international trade, and they looked back with envy to the easier pre-war world. Perhaps their nostalgia blunted their understanding, even their memories, of what had happened before 1914. They were certainly too ready to ascribe the pre-war successes of Britain as an export economy to the international gold standard. The Bank of England and American bankers had learned to maintain a gold standard by sharp variations in short-term rates of interest, while such rates were fairly stable in the great financial centres on the Continent of Europe. Whether this way of running the world's monetary systems made more for stability than for instability of prices and production is one of the unanswered—perhaps unanswerable—questions of economic history. But in 1925 British authorities thought they knew the answer, and with a restored gold standard the country entered on a period of monetary difficulty that has with some variation lasted ever since.

Part of the answer may be that monetary conditions hardly ever mattered greatly, and that both the underlying upward trend in productivity and the cyclical ups and downs in activity and income were dependent at once on deep-rooted, slowly maturing changes in technique, in population, and in social conditions, and on the accidents of timing that occasionally seem to make everything change at once. The change in the tempo of economic growth in England around 1895-1900—from a faster to a slower growth—has been one of the puzzles of a later generation which has been more 'growth-conscious'. Maybe the answer is to be found in the mere expiry of a fortunate coincidence of results—during the previous thirty years—of much earlier inventiveness and enterprise. The coincidences are not always so fortunate, and in the late 'twenties and early 'thirties things seemed rather to conspire to defeat every effort to maintain, let alone advance, the prosperity of the English people. Yet at that very time, the standard of living of the *employed* men and their families was, thanks to cheaper imports, rising faster than it had risen for many decades.

By 1930 it was clear enough that no wishful thinking would take the English economy back to 1913. Nor indeed, by the time 1930 came round, did most thinking Englishmen have any desire to go back to 1913. 'The world turns and the world changes', and in the economic environment change was visible enough to prompt men to ask themselves some probing questions—including some of the unanswerables. At the opening of the period 1880-1939, John Stuart Mill was the leading English economist. He was the first to play sympathetically with socialistic notions; but this aspect of his thought was not developed by Alfred Marshall, who was in the ascendant at the end of the century and dominated English economic thought through the greater part of the period. 'Let the State be up and doing', said Marshall in 1907, but his main contribution to the written body of economic thought was a mathematician's development (in Book V of his *Principles*) of analysis of the price system in a world of small and freely competing firms. As it happened, the changing structure of industry was already driving this Marshallian world into the past, though Marshallian treatment of monopoly as the exception in a flexible and competitive world coloured the first political approach to the problem of monopoly in 1917-20. After that, for a few years men hankered (unreasonably, as it seems to us now) after a return to 1913, but by the end of the 'twenties reflection on the first post-war decade—and especially the paradox of poverty in the midst of plenty—helped to bring about a major change in the climate of economic thought. The economic cataclysm of 1930-3, which England shared with the whole world, gave the final impetus to this change. J. M. Keynes, the greatest economist in his generation, led the way in a revolution in his subject, justifying a major extension in the economic role of government. Before this revolution found its reflection in economic policy, however, there was a cataclysm of a different kind. Back in 1924 Keynes had prophesied, in his famous lecture *The End of Laisser Faire*, that 'the fiercest contests and the most deeply felt divisions of opinion are likely to be waged in the coming years not round technical questions, where the arguments on either side are mainly economic, but round those which, for want of better words, may be called psychological or, perhaps, moral'. He spoke more truly than he knew, for the pitiful economic experience

of the 'thirties was to be ended in an ideological World War. When
at long last that was over, the English people turned to explore more
consciously the management of the Mixed Economy, to enjoy the
fruits of its expansion, and to ponder the questions that it posed.

A Note on Further Reading

THE ONLY COMPREHENSIVE COVERAGE of the subject is by W. Ashworth, *An Economic History of England, 1870-1939* (1960), an excellent book which the student should read at an early stage and may continue to use for reference. J. H. Clapham, *An Economic History of Modern Britain*, vol. 3 (1938), is important for the earlier part of the period; it becomes patchy after 1900 and has little to say on post-1914. For this period a great deal of factual material will be found in S. Pollard, *The Development of the British Economy, 1914-50* (1962); while W. A. Lewis, *Economic Survey, 1919-1939* (1949) is probably the most helpful of a number of works which discuss the international scene.

For reference to statistics, there is the invaluable *Abstract of British Historial Statistics* edited by B. R. Mitchell with the collaboration of Phyllis Deane (1962). A much smaller collection, produced by the London and Cambridge Economic Service for *The Times Review of Industry and Technology*, is *Key Statistics of the British Economy 1900-1962* (no date).

A wide range of subjects, especially relating to the subject-matter of my Chapters 2, 6, and 8, is covered by the papers of the *Committee on Industry and Trade* (the Balfour Committee). The *Final Report* (1929) of this Committee is unexciting, but during the years 1925-8 it published a series of volumes on overseas trade, various groups of industries, and industrial relations, which are the best reference works covering the early 1920s and are useful for historical sketches reaching back into the previous century. The student should also learn to use, for searching out the vast body of other official papers of the inter-war period, P. Ford and G. Ford, *A Breviate of Parliamentary Papers 1917-1939* (1951).

On population questions, an exceptionally well-qualified Royal Commission issued its *Report* (Cmd. 7695) in 1949; its other papers may be used for reference. The student should also learn to use the reports of the decennial census of population, which include occupational as well as many other analyses.

On overseas trade, S. B. Saul, *Studies in Overseas Trade, 1870-1914* (1960) is an excellent book, without which the discussion in my Chapter 2 would not have been possible. R. J. S. Hoffman, *Great Britain and the German Trade Rivalry, 1875-1914* (1933), deals with an important aspect of the subject in the same period. Clapham (cited above) is particularly interesting on overseas trade but stops short of the final decades; on these A. E. Kahn, *Great Britain in the World Economy* (1946) should be consulted. On economic fluctuations the summary analysis of the facts, used in Chapters 3 and 4 of this book, is most succinctly presented by J. H. Wilson, in his Appendix A to W. H. Beveridge, *Full Employment in a Free Society* (1944). Chapter I of Clapham's Vol. 3 (see above) is useful for pre-1914; so is A. K. Cairncross, *Home and Foreign Investment, 1870-1913* (1953). For war and post-war, see E. V. Morgan, *Studies in British Financial Policy, 1918-1925* (1947), and A. C. Pigou, *Aspects of British Economic History, 1918-1925* (1947). Throughout the period—and for more general purposes than the study of the trade cycle—reference may be made to the (annual) *Commercial History and Review* issued with *The Economist*, but the student must allow for its disproportionately great interest in foreign trade and its strong attachment to Free Trade doctrine.

The performance of the British economy before 1914 is treated in W. W. Rostow, *The British Economy in the Nineteenth Century* (1948) and in a considerable number of articles by various authors. Of these the following are the most important: E. H. Phelps Brown and D. Handfield-Jones, 'The Climacteric of the 1890s: a study in an Expanding Economy', *Oxford Economic Papers* (N.S.), 1952; D. J. Coppock, 'The Climacteric of the 1890s: a Critical Note', *Manchester School*, XXIV, 1956; and H. W. Richardson, 'Retardation in Britain's Industrial Growth, 1870-1913', *Scottish Journal of Political Economy*, XII, 1965.

There has been little systematic study as yet of the new industries treated in Chapter 5, except in occasional articles in periodicals (see below), but readers at every stage will find W. H. G. Armytage, *A Social History of Engineering* (1961) lively and stimulating; his Chapters 16-22 are particularly relevant. J. H. Dunning and C. J. Thomas, *British Industry; Change and Development in the Twentieth Century* (1961) is a useful introductory study, as also is A. Plummer, *New British Industries in the Twentieth Century* (1937). The old industries (my Chapter 6) had much attention in the Balfour Committee *Surveys* (see above). For coal see also the first chapter of W. H. B. Court's volume *Coal* (1951) in the official *History of the Second World War* series, and the *Report of the Royal Commission on the Coal Industry* (1925) (Samuel Commission), which is probably the best threepennyworth published by H.M. Stationery Office in the last half-century. Duncan Burn, *The Economic History of Steel-making 1867-1939* is a standard work: S. G. Sturmey, *British Shipping and World Competition* (1962) and M. E. A. Bowley, *Housing and the State* (1945) should also be consulted. A. F. Lucas, *Industrial Reconstruction and the Control of Competition* (1937) is a useful inter-war view of a variety of British industries, old and new. There are many histories of firms, the most notable being C. Wilson, *The History of Unilever* (1954). For agricultural history (Chapter 7), C. S. Orwin and E. H. Whetham, *History of British Agriculture 1846-1914* (1964) and F. M. L. Thomson, *English Landed*

Society in the Nineteenth Century (1963) cover the earlier part of the period. For the inter-war years a useful reference book is W. Astor and B. S. Rowntree (eds.), *British Agriculture* (1938).

For conditions of labour, industrial relations, etc. (Chapter 8), much the most stimulating book is E. H. Phelps Brown, *The Growth of Industrial Relations* (1959); it is mostly concerned with 1906-14 and is distinguished for its unusual combination of scholarly independence and human sympathy. On trade unionism as such, apart from the standard work by Sidney and Beatrice Webb, H. M. Pelling, *A History of British Trade Unionism* (1963) is an excellent modern introductory study. A larger recent work is H. A. Clegg and others, *A History of British Trade Unionism since 1889*, Vol. I *1889-1910* (1964). Lord Amulree, *Industrial Arbitration in Great Britain* (1929) is more specialized but includes the 1920s as well as pre-war. See also the Balfour Committee *Survey* noted above.

The material relating to Chapters 9 and 10 of this book is widely scattered over many of the sources noted above, official reports, the periodical literature, etc. Special mention should perhaps be made of H. D. Henderson, *The Inter-War Years* (1955), a collection of contemporary papers in which the reader can perceive the change in the climate of economic thought as it was taking place; the book is also a useful source on monetary history. The specialized literature of monetary history also includes an interesting biography, H. Clay, *Lord Norman* (1957), which incidentally includes some sidelights on the industrial history of the 1920s.

In the periodical literature, the reader will find most of the important articles in the *Economic History Review* and *Business History*. Of these, *Business History* (published by the University of Liverpool Press) has the narrower range, but a greater proportion of articles relevant to the period of this book. The *Economic History Review* is the journal of the Economic History Society, which has a reduced subscription rate for students. This Society has sponsored three volumes of reprinted articles, *Essays in Economic History* (ed. E. Carus-Wilson), of which the first and third contain articles on this period. (The two classic articles by H. A. Shannon on the early limited liability companies are included in Vol. I.) *The Yorkshire Bulletin of Economic and Social Research* in May 1965 published a special issue (Vol. 17, no. i) entitled *Studies in the British Economy 1870-1914* (ed. John Saville).

Index

The Index does not include references to the names in the Note on Further Reading